THE BLACK MAN IN
AND ITS

THE BLACK MAN IN THE OLD TESTAMENT AND ITS WORLD

A Study of the Facts that are Revealed in the Authorized (King James) Version of the Holy Bible during the Days in Which the Old Testament Was Lived

Bishop Alfred G. Dunston, Jr.

Africa World Press, Inc.

P.O. Box 1892
Trenton, New Jersey 08607

Africa World Press Inc.

P.O. Box 1892
Trenton, NJ 08607

Copyright © 1992 Alfred G. Dunston, Jr .
First Africa World Press Edition, 1992
Second Printing, 1993
Third Printing, 1994

Book design and typesetting by Malcolm Litchfield
This book composed in Palatino and Univers

Cover Design and illustration by Carles J. Juzang

Library of Congress Catalog Card Number: 91-78315

ISBN: 0-86543-304-6   *Cloth*
        0-86543-305-4   *Paper*

To my daughters

**Carol Jean Goodrich
Aingred Ghislaine James
Dr. Armayne Garrinetta Dunston**

Good children help parents to be good ones.

CONTENTS

PREFACE

I N THE FOLLOWING PAGES, there is an attempt to produce the type of book that is greatly needed and has been needed for a very long time; for the presence of the black man on the Old Testament scene is a subject that has not heretofore proved to be inviting to many writers. There is not much bibliography to be found that deals with the subject comprehensively, and the author cannot claim to have found all the material that is available; hence, the subject matter that is contained in this little volume has been drawn from many scattered sources. Some of the facts to which attention is now called have been shared in sermons, lectures, seminars, and in conference institute sessions for several years. Friends and advisors agree that the time has come to lay out certain facts in a systematic order so that the whole picture can be seen.

This study is based upon the words of the Old Testament as they are given to us in the Authorized (King James) Version of the Holy Bible. Other translations have been used for references and clarification. Such versions as the Revised Standard Version and the Dartmouth Bible have been indispensably helpful, but the authority always rests upon what is projected in the translation called for by King James for the better enlightenment of English speaking people. And it should be noted that other versions and translations of the Holy Bible into English give us the same treatment of the same material that we find in the King James Version on the subject of the present study. We must all continue to await the day when truly capable scholars will delve into the original languages of the Bible and bring forth additional light upon the subject that is dealt with within the following pages. There is no dearth of biblical scholars. Fortunately for the church, there are many men and women within the Christian community who are very capable of searching their way through all the various translations of the ages. If they will do so, these people have the talent and education that are needed to unearth myriads of historic truths that bear directly upon the subject of the black man's participation in the Old Testament world. So far the writers have barely "scratched the surface," but it is known that great treasuries of facts are locked away in places wherein only the most highly trained scholars can enter and probe and weigh and interpret. This book does not attempt to be the last word on the subject, but it does try to bring forth a world view of the subject as it is reflected in the history that touches the Old Testament.

Since the opening years of the sixteenth century, Christian biblical scholarship has been the ally of racism, sometimes deliberately and sometimes unconsciously. The alliance has run the gamut from avid support of the black inferiority myth to a mere indifference to the situation; and at both extremes, the racial myths have found growing room. In all likelihood there are millions of Christians today who still believe that the curse of Noah fell upon the black man. This fallacy was once taught by leading scholars and writers of their day, and the successors of those scholars and writers have done very little to erase the fallacy. Secular writers have done more to correct these myths than biblical ones; and this is possibly one of the reasons that many young black Americans call the Holy Scripture "the white man's Bible."

This book attempts to do something that should have been done at least four hundred years ago. It attempts to portray the black man as he was viewed during the Old Testament times. The facts are all there, and some of them are herein brought to attention. It is our hope that this is only the beginning of a procession of books on the subject, because the author makes no claim to have exhausted the topic. This is meant to be a textbook for those who wish to become learners in the field, and to help build a better self-image for those who need it. Hopefully, it will also open the eyes of others whose minds have been beclouded. The chapters on the histories of Egypt and Cush (or Kush) deal with them in a cursory manner, except when details are necessary to the point at labor, and some of the analyses of the Scripture passages will enrich the student's knowledge of the Bible.

This author is grateful to his secretary, Miss Julia Murphy, who typed and corrected a great deal of the spelling, and to The Rev. Vaughn Thomas Eason, president, and Dr. John H. Satterwhite, dean of The Institute For Black Ministries, for giving me the opportunity to offer a course bearing the name of this book. The members of the South Alabama, Central Alabama, West Central North Carolina, and the North Carolina Annual Conferences of the African Methodist Episcopal Zion Church have greatly encouraged the author. These are the Annual Conferences in which the author presides; and when told that the book was forthcoming, they seemed eager to have it finished so that they could read it.

1

THE TERM "NEGRO"

NEGRO IS A TERM that has come to be very passionately hated by many of the young black people of the United States, but at the same time it is dearly beloved by some white people, and especially by certain white writers. Many young blacks hate the term, because to them it represents slavery, subjugation, docility, and white contempt. They have been led to believe that the term denotes a low type of human being who accepts the indignities heaped upon him by white racism and whose individual pride has been broken to the point that he conceives of himself as being inferior to whites and a fit object of their domination. On the other hand, many white American writers love the term because it apparently symbolizes for them the myth of black inferiority and is a constant reminder of the days when nothing prevented whites from treading upon black bondmen at will. In strange psychological ways, the term "Negro" to many white people is a code word actually meaning "someone who I am better than." This is an element of those "odious peculiarities" of which Thomas Jefferson warned the United States of his day.

The group of young black Americans now under consideration experience no change in attitude when they are told that before and during the early thirties, there was a great discussion in the black community on the question of what Afro-Americans wanted to be called. However, such discussion did take place in high school and college classrooms, in homes and organized groups of the communities; in barber shops and beauty parlors, and in other gathering places, including the churches. The Afro-Americans of that period quite definitely did not want to be called "colored," because such a term was far too general, and included, in their judgement, the whole world of non-white people. They rejected the term in the firm conviction that the black people of the United States had become a distinct ethnic and national group of people in the world. "The Negro National Anthem" was committed to memory, and it was sung with an emotion too deep to be understood by their present-day descendants. The response of that day to the greatest of all modern songs came from the depth of feeling that could build a pride never to be shaken.

During these days just described, the term "black," was utterly rejected as something to call someone. Millions were as black then as they are now, but still the word black symbolized ugliness, and it did not technically describe black people with lighter complexions. The blackest lady in any community, when called "black," might quickly report, "I ain't black." Terms like "brown," "sepia," and "tan" were adopted by the black media in order not to offend the mood. So the generations of the twenties and thirties chose first of all to be called "Afro-Americans," but they also chose to be called "Negroes," because that term applied to a race or nation of people in the United States of America whose ancestors came from Africa and who thereby possessed African "blood." This was their thinking. They were proud of the strength, stamina and character that had shown through in spite of the chains that bound their fathers. They recounted over and over the story of the progress that their fathers had made in spite of slavery, brutality and discrimination, and they decided that it was honorable to be called what the fathers had been called. They spent years and years fighting with the white press on the matter of capitalizing the term "Negro" whenever it was used, and they protested in order to get the white southerner to stop pronouncing the word "Nigra"; and all black blood boiled with fury when a white person used the term "Nigger," or when a black person used the term within hearing distance of white ears. An older generation still feels that the term "Negro" is too honorable to be derided, because those who lived under that name built a race and an honorable nationhood.

European writers in general avoid all use of the term "Negro" when writing about Africans and African history. They never use the term because, having lived there, they know obviously that the term when applied to Africa is completely unscientific, and that it identifies nobody on the African continent at all. European writers are in no way or part responsible for any idea that would cause a black American to say, "I'm not a Negro; there is a Negro tribe in Africa, but I am not one of them." The false basis for such a type of statement comes from the United States, South America and the West Indies. These European writers understand that Africans are called by ethnic group names-groups that are mistakenly called "tribes."

The author looked up the term "Negro" in Webster's dictionary forty-five years ago because of a boyhood discussion of its meaning, and the definition that was found then is the same that is rendered in the *New Century Dictionary* of today:

Negro (Sp. and Pg. Negro, black, as N. a black person, Negro L. Niger, black) 1. N; pl. Negroes (groz) also L.C. A member of a black skinned people; (also L.C.) a person having more or less Negro blood; specif. (sometimes L.C.) a member of the Negro or black race (see below) II a (also

L.C.) belonging to a black skinned people (as, "The first Negro slaves were brought to Jamestown in Virginia by a Dutch ship as early as 1620." H.G. Wells "Outline of History; XXXVIII 2; (also L.C.) inhabited by Negroes; specif. (sometimes L.C.) noting or pertaining to the so called "black" race; characterized chiefly by a black complexion, short broad and flat nose, projecting jaws, thick lips, and crisp or woolly hair, and generally regarded as embracing the native inhabitants of the *Sudan Senegambia,* and the region southward to the vicinity of the equator, and their descendants elsewhere, but sometimes considered to include also many other African Tribes further South.

Thus the term "Negro" is a Spanish-Portuguese term, coming from the Latin root "Niger," both of which mean "black"; and from the Latin "Niger" also comes from the French "Noir" and the Italian "Nero." This Spanish-Portuguese term was borrowed by the English (and all Europe) in mid-sixteenth century,[1] and was used to designate all African people living to the south of Egypt and the Sahara Desert. The term "Negro" as applied to Africa had no further derivation or meaning, and Basil Davidson[2] speaks of the Greek view of "all those people who lived, lost in mystery, in Africa beyond Egypt"; these Africans they called Ethiopians—rather as later Europeans would indiscriminantly call them "Negroes." It should be added that the term is not found at all in ancient records.

When the Europeans applied the term "Negroes," they were designating blacks who lived south of the Sahara. Generally, these people have distinctive physical characteristics that vary in all respects, but Europe used the term to designate skin color along with geography. Other physical features such as the shape of the nose or wooliness of hair or thickness of lips did not change the general designation, and can have no significance today in the vain attempt to decide which African is Negro and which is not. While those physical features mentioned above are generally characteristic of myriads of people, they can never be used to determine any particular group living south of the Sahara and between the Atlantic and Indian oceans. In black Africa, a people's shade of black has no ethnic significance.

Writers who wander around in the maze of physical differences found in sub-Saharan Africa (and largely on the North African littoral) trying to designate some as Hamitic (term of no ethnic significance), some as Nilotic (meaning of or pertaining to the Nile river or the inhabitants of its region) some as bushmanoid, some as Caucasoid and some as Negroid or Negro are following a pattern that is at best unscientific and at worst is absolutely ridiculous.

There are no "true Negroes" in any part of sub-Saharan Africa, nor in North Africa. Color shades vary in all parts of Africa. Cranial features vary in all parts of Africa. Lip and nose shape vary in all parts of Africa. Other physical features also vary in all parts of Africa. Repeat: There are no "true Negroes" in sub-Saharan Africa. If the term "Negro" can possibly be used at all in Africa, then scientific procedure must be forsaken and the name applied to black Africa as a whole—from the steppes of the Sahara to the Cape of Good Hope, and from ocean to ocean. Paul Bohannon[3] sums up the whole matter of race in Africa by saying, "Race, in short, is in the eye of the beholder"; and he earlier says, "Today we can say little more than this: if one stands at Suez and looks South and Southwest, people tend to get darker the further one goes."

Anyone who has proper respect for Africans and their civilization will not call them Negroes. They have bitterly rejected the term in the past, and they do so today. To the African the term "Negroes" applies to the black man in the Americas, and, incidentally, prior to the years when men like Nkrumah and Azikiwe returned to West Africa from studying in England and the United States, most of their people were not even aware of their kinship to black Americans. They had studied about them in schools at home, but the relationship had not been explained. Furthermore, during the entire period of European Colonialism in Africa, their records designated people by their tribal ethnic names. The term "negroid" is both revolting and insulting, because it seeks to make a separate species of human beings who have certain cranial and facial traits. The color difference between people of extremes is unsound enough, and to divide and designate people within any color group according to the thickness of their lips or the wooliness of the hair or the size and shape of the noses, is repugnant to science and reason. When someone unearths a three-thousand-year-old fossil skull and from that skull pretends to determine that the once-living creature had "negroid" features, it is then time for such person to find another field of endeavor.

This new troublesome term "Negro" crossed the ocean with the Atlantic slave trade, and was used to designate all darker-than-white people who were kidnapped and sold from anywhere in Africa, Madagascar, Zanzibar, etc. Winthrop Jordan[4] cites a passage from the diary of Samuel Seward in 1709, telling of a black Spaniard who petitioned the Massachusetts Council for his freedom, and was turned down when "Captain Teat alleged that all of that color were slaves." There is also the case of a woman who sued at court to regain her freedom on the basis that she was from Madagascar, and it is known that the slave trade involved small groups of captives from Arabia and possibly elsewhere.

Another new term appeared in the American colonies sometime around 1680, and that the new term was "white." It had not been used in Europe apparently because there was no appreciable amount of contrasting color.

In the West Indies and South America, the term "Negro" has had a different meaning than in the United States. John Gunther,[5] writing about Brazil, says this: "The country is . . . sixty percent white, fifteen percent Negro, and twenty-five percent half-caste. But white is an extremely loose and indeterminate term; there are all manner and varieties of white, ranging from cream and alabaster to deepest olive; actually a great many 'whites' have a touch at least of Negro blood."

Gunther says further, "The Portuguese had no aversion to physical contact with African women; . . . one old saying is that the Portuguese used white women for marriage, mulattoes for sex, Negroes for work; a variant of this is the description of seventeenth century Brazil as 'a hell for blacks, a purgatory for whites, and a paradise for mulattoes.'"

In another place Gunther says of Brazil that discrimination does exist, even if outright segregation does not. "The darker the skin, the worse the treatment. Negroes become relegated to the lowest class of work in the big cities." In Brazil, he says, "color is deceptive. A man white as white will tell you that he has a Negro grandparent."

A contrast in the colonialization of the West Indies with that of the United States is shown in a statement taken from Life World Library:[6] "The Europeans operated the island plantations and their slave workers as commercial properties. . . . The colonists were rough men who went out to the tropics for a limited period to make their fortune. . . . They made their money in the islands and spent it grandly in the cities of Europe, where 'rich as a West Indies Planter' became a common phrase." In the next paragraph it is stated that the planters "had no reluctance in taking the prettier (black) girls as sexual partners and even as established concubines. Inevitably many of these men developed affection for their women and for their children. . . . As a result, another class, free people of mixed parentage, came into exis- tence. . . . In the English Islands they were called 'Free Colored' or simply 'Colored People.' In the French Islands they were known as *gens de coleur* or *Affranchic* (freed ones); in the Spanish Islands, where color has been of less importance, they were referred to as *Libertos* or *Emancipados*." The final World Library quotation says, "European ancestry is, for obvious reasons in a onetime slave society, a desirable possession, even in small proportions, and is claimed whenever possible. Negro ancestry is denied when appearances permit. . . . The 'lowest class' generally consists of rural laborers with dark skins and limited education. The next 'higher' is made up of urban professionals of mixed European and African ancestry."

These references point to the truth that in South America and in the West Indies the term "Negro" included only the persons that are actually black in complexion or whose skin complexion showed a minimum amount of racial mixture. People of African descent whose complexions showed obvious racial mixtures were not referred to as Negroes, but were referred to in other terms. These designations are in force today in the places mentioned, and because of the socio-racial history of South America and the West Indian islands, the people with black or dark complexions were and still are on the bottom of the social and economic scale in most instances.

This condition infuriated Marcus Garvey, and he therefore crusaded against "coloreds" as well as against whites; and among his followers in the United States there were many who held prejudice against the lighter-skinned Afro-Americans.The black-skinned people in South America and the West Indies have been a singularly abused lot. The situation has changed greatly with the passing of time, but the separation of African descendants by skin color is still a very real fact to the South of the United States.

The colonial history of the United States has differed from that of South America and the Indies, because the United States was from the beginning a haven for Europe's poor and distressed who were seeking permanent homes for their families. They were strictly colonists rather than soldiers of fortune or planter-speculators. They left Europe, and there was little or nothing to which they could return because their shallow roots had been severed, and in most instances they brought their families with them or sent back for them when land was secured, as did the Boers of South Africa. In cases where they met and married in America, they were forced to marry their own color. Colonial law prohibited marriage between blacks and whites, and the effect of the law was strengthened when the white wives of black men were put into slavery and the white husbands of black concubines were severely punished. In 1691, the Virginia Assembly denounced all interracial unions and the children born thereto as "that abominable mixture and spurious issue."

Clandestine cohabitation between white males and black females was tolerated to the point of encouragement in the early United States. One more indelible blot on American moral history lay in the fact that myriads of white men enslaved and sold into further enslavement their own sons and daughters begotten of black women. For the next ten thousand years, ethicists and moralists will be trying to explain the kind of individual or racial debasement that would allow a human being to enslave and sell into enslavement to others those that were his own flesh and blood; but they can never explain it so as to make it honorable.

In colonial America, as today, the term "Negro" has meant "individuals of a group who are of pure African descent or any degree of admixture of 'Negro' blood with any other race or races."[7] This definition includes a person called mulatto, which is described in a Virginia law of 1705 as "the child of an Indian, and the child, grandchild, or great grandchild of a Negro."[8]

Around 1705, the state of North Carolina (typifying all the states) designated as "Negro" all persons having one-eighth to one-sixteenth African blood,[9] and North Carolina was considered one of the more enlightened states in the colonies. The colonial states of the United States borrowed from the West Indies such terms as "Maroons," "Mulattoes," "Octoroons," and "Quadroons," solely to describe complexions and to use in the slave trade, but all laws decreed that they were of Negro status. The laws that forbade black and white marriages drove interracial sex somewhat underground, and made it utterly impossible for even the most powerful white man to gain legitimacy for his sexual union with a black woman or the offsprings therefrom. Such offspring could not inherit as children and descendants, and there was for them no higher social level over the darker brother. The lighter-skinned Afro-American is a black person with a light complexion.

The Afro-Americans who gained freedom and sometimes fortune got it through Revolutionary War service, service in the War of 1812, self-purchase, being purchased by a mate , conscience-strickenness of some slaveholders, and exceptionally meritorious service to the slavecrats in some manner. Color and skin complexion had little to do with the acquisition of freedom and fortune, and those bondmen who gained freedom ran the entire scale of skin complexions; in conceding with Benjamin Brawley, the mulatto group gained it faster.

Historically then, all Afro-Americans have lived under the same status. Benjamin Brawley cites a Virginia law enacted in 1705 saying that no "Negro, Mulatto, or Indian shall from and after the publication of this act bear any office ecclesiastical, civil or military, or be in any place of public trust or power. . . ." The Afro-American child born to a white parent has been a Negro. The Afro-American children born to an American Indian, or Chinese, etc., have been Negro. The African descendants in U.S. Territory have all been enslaved together, have suffered under segregation together, been discriminated against, brutalized, lynched, and called "Niggers" together. Complexion made no difference for the African descendant. Carl Sandburg[10] tells of an Alabama planter who advertised: "Run away-Alfred, a bright mulatto boy, working on plantation; about 18 years old, pretty well grown, has blue eyes, light flaxen hair, skin exposed to freckle; he will try to pass as Freeborn." Another planter advertised: "One hundred dollars reward for return of a bright mulatto slave, named Sam; light sandy hair, blue eyes, ruddy complexion, is so white as very easily to pass for a free white man."

Frederick Douglas, the great abolitionist who became famous on two continents, escaped from slavery posing as white. Benjamin Quarles[11] (and most black history writers) describes the flight of a slave couple, William and Ellen Craft, who fled from Macon, Georgia, to the free North while she posed as a hard-of-hearing, arm-in-sling, ailing planter going North for medical treatment, carrying her male slave nurse with her.

It would be a colossal disaster for the Afro-American to allow his race to be divided either on the basis of skin complexion or whatever term is used to designate the race or the individual. A brutal history has made them one, and the country has never shown any preference for one complexion over another; it would be tragic to encourage such attitudes now. To be sure, certain individuals have shown preferences of complexion, and so have some groups, families, organizations and villages, but these are individual and personal preferences. The American society has treated all the same. They are all one—the black, the jet black, the very black, the near black, the off-black, the brown, the sepia, the tan, the "merigny," the red, the dirty red, the white, the yallah and the high yallah. (The word "yellow" was never used in black culture to describe a light-skin person. Even in the darkest days, black people knew the meaning of yellow and could at least pronounce it "yillow" even in dialect. Even to this day in black southern culture, if a Ph.D. is going to use the term at all, he will not say "yellow" but "yallah.")

Black forebears worked in the same fields, were lynched on the same trees, were broken on the same wheels, were beheaded by the same slave-catching patrols; they ran towards freedom together, and married each other regardless of complexion. Their history has made them one nation, one people having a common destiny, fighting in courts, tramping in freedom marches, sitting at lunch counters; protesting, demonstrating, agitating, writing, preaching, praying, singing, shouting, looking for certain victory.

The black Martinique poet Aime Cesaire exulted in his "negritude," and more than forty years before this date, a black man named Langston Hughes, who was almost white in complexion, wrote these lines: "I'm A Negro, Black Like The Night Is Black."

Questions

1. What is the definition of the term "Negro"?
2. What people were designated "Negroes" by the Europeans?
3. Where are the true Negroes found in Africa?

4. Which Africans accept the name Negroes for themselves?
5. Why should the term "negroid" be rejected?
6. What brought the term "Negro" to the Americas?
7. When did the term "white man" appear in the American colonies?
8. What people are called Negroes in South America?
9. What people are called Negroes in the West Indies?
10. What people are called Negroes in the U.S.A.?
11. How did Afro-Americans gain freedom during slavery days?

Notes

1. Winthrop D. Jordan, *White Over Black* (Williamsburg, Va: University of North Carolina Press, 1968), p. 61.
2. Basil Davidson, *Africa: History of a Continent* (New York: Macmillan, 1966), p. 36.
3. Paul Bohannon, *Africa and Africans* (New York: Natural History Press, 1964), p. 68. Bohannon further states that there is not an undisputed "line that can be drawn on a map, or distinctions that can be made between tribes (in other than statistical terms) with the claim that one is unequivocally Caucasoid and the other Negroid. In even the most dominantly Negroid tribe, there are to be found individuals with light skins and green eyes; in the northern regions of Africa, there are some people with dark skins and kinky hair."
4. *Ibid.*
5. John Gunther, *Inside South America* (New York: Harper & Row, 1966), p. 8.
6. Carter Herman and the editors of *Life*, *The West Indies* (New York: Time, Inc., 1963), p. 13.
7. *Encyclopedia Americana*, 1953 Edition, Vol. 1.
8. Benjamin Brawley, *A Social History of the American Negro* (London: Collier-Macmillan Ltd., 1921), p. 28.
9. Jordan, *White over Black*, p. 169.
10. Sandburg's Abraham Lincoln contains many similar stories.
11. The story of William and Ellen Craft is recounted by most of the writers in black history.

2

WHAT THE BIBLE MEANS BY THE TERM "ETHIOPIA"

THE TERM "ETHIOPIA" (or Ethiopian) is used almost from the beginning to the end of the Holy Bible, and its usage continues to mislead millions of people who think that the Ethiopia of today and the Ethiopia of the Bible are the same; but such is not the case at all.

The Ethiopia which appears on modern maps has had a very long existence indeed, and it is descended from the Axumite Empire which is said to date from the eighteenth century of the pre-Christian Era. The Axumite Nation as such is not mentioned in the records of the Old Testament times. The first written knowledge of it comes to us through the writings of an unidentified Greek mariner around 60 A.D. He wrote a periplus of the Erythraean Sea, which was meant as a guide to both trade and navigation in the Red Sea and in the Indian Ocean. The periplus describes the seaport city of Adulis, which once belonged to the

Kingdom of Axum but is now located in the country of Eritrea. In the periplus the Axumite king is called Zocales.

The Ethiopians of the modern map claim descent from the ancient kingdom of Saba, which is located in what is now South Arabia, and historians have found that South Arabians did cross the Red Sea and colonize this portion of Africa at some point in time around the fifth century before the coming of Christ.

The Abyssinians (modern Ethiopians) therefore do not regard themselves as wholly African people, and this is supported by their language, which is said to be Semitic. They are a mixture of black Africa, Somali, Gallo and Yemen, and their civilization is perhaps best described by calling it a Sabaen-African civilization.

Modern Ethiopians, we are told, fiercely resent being called black, possibly because of the Semitic and other strains in their background. Their land became recognized by the European powers in 1896 as the Kingdom of Abyssinia after they defeated the Italian army at Adowa. The name "Abyssinia" is said by one source to have grown out of a Muslim term, "habeshi" (meaning mixed), which was a scornful name for Christians, but "the people, however, have clung to the older name of Ethiopia for their country."[1] Another source says that the term Abyssinia is the Portuguese form of the Arabian term "habesch," meaning "mixture."[2]

The Sabaens are mentioned in the Book of Job, and Sheba (or Seba) is mentioned in several other places. It has been established that the famed Queen of Sheba of Solomanic times came from Saba in Arabia, although many people, like Josephus the Jewish historian, thought that she came from Africa. An interval of many centuries makes impossible the cherished myth that the Meneliks descended from a union of Soloman and Sheba, but the "Lion of Judah" continued to hold fast to his claim.

The marginal notes of the English Bible always translate the word "Ethiopia" to "Kush" or "Cush," and rightly so. Ethiopia is a Greek term, and is the name which they applied to the lands south of Egypt. The marginal translations begin in Genesis 2:13, and here the marginal notes translate the term "Ethiopia" as meaning "Cush" in the Hebrew language. This does not mean that "Cush" is a Hebrew term, for it was not. The name Cush (or Kush) was given by Egypt to her southern neighbor, and the name so appeared in Egyptian records. This and other such marginal references make it appear certain that in pre-Grecian times the Hebrew Scriptures called the land "Cush"; and according to Josephus, the Jewish historian, this name was used in all Asia.

The Grecian custom of referring to Cush as Ethiopia was carried evidently into nineteenth century literature, and by then it had become the permanent name among Europeans. This can be discovered in the opera *Aïda*, which was written by Giuseppi Verdi and first produced in Cairo, Egypt, in 1871. The libretto (the words) are attributed to Camille du Locle and Antonio Ghislanzoni, whose part of the work was based upon a sketch by one Mariette Bey, supposedly an Egyptologist. The plot for *Aïda* is the story of a war between Egypt and Ethiopia, but the secret route of the planned invasion by Egypt would go by way of Napata. The city of Napata has always been located in the Sudan beyond the third cataract of the Nile River, and it was the first capital of the Cushite kings. The city is still shown on some maps of the area.

Ethiopia is a Greek term meaning "burnt faces," and was obviously applied by the Greeks because of the skin color of the inhabitants of the Sudan. It must have come into the Hebrew Bible with the Septuagint translation by the Greek scholars. Herodotus (and other Greek writers) spoke glowingly well of the people whom he called Ethiopians, as will be noted later; but these people are among the very few nations or peoples in history, literature, or in Scripture that have been named according to their skin color.

The same nation that was called Cush by the Egyptians and ancient Hebrews, was called Ethiopia by the Greeks and Nubia by the Christians, after Julian planted the faith there during the sixth century A.D.

Islam began its conquest in the area later than 700 A.D., and by the fourteenth or fifteenth century had made itself the only and official religion of the area. Fortunately for latter day students, the Arab Muslims, in following the prior custom of renaming conquered places, used a term that is more unmistakably descriptive than the Greek term. They called it "Bilad as Sudan," an Arab term meaning "land of the blacks." This name was applied to "the whole vast space of Steppe and Savanna that lies between the Sahara and the forest lands further to south, an area that stretches from the Atlantic at Dakar all the way across Africa to the Red Sea, and covers as much as a thousand miles from North to South."[3]

Later Europeans called the Sudanese people "Negroes," and the term applied to all the then-known people south of Egypt and the Sahara, as is more fully explained in Chapter 1.

It is at this point that the forty-seven active King James translators performed a definite disservice to the Christian church in general, and to the black African and his descendants in particular. Their rendering of this particular area of translation in some sense might have contributed to the continuing scourge of slavery that mars the pages of Western world history, because Western consciences might possibly have reacted differently had the biblical Ethiopians been more closely identified.

The King James Version was completed and presented to the king in the year 1611 A.D. Their presentation speech praised the king and gave to him the full credit for having seen the need for such a work as that which they were presenting. According to their speech, the king saw the need for "one more exact translation of the Holy Scriptures into the English tongue." They declared that they had given to the English-speaking people precisely that which the king desired for them. The speech is replete with pious language, and we hear them saying of themselves that they had "walked in ways of simplicity and integrity." They saw themselves as poor instruments "to make

God's Holy truths to be yet more and more known unto the
people."

Their own explanations say that the King James translators
worked out of "original sacred tongues," and compared other
translations; and there is evidence that they desired to make
various texts and accounts more understandable to English
people. For example, in setting down the lineage of Esau, the
English Bible says that there were "Dukes" among the sons of
Esau. We all know that the ancient Hebrew gave us no term that
actually corresponds with the term "duke," but in the eyes of
Europeans generally and the English particularly, the royal place
and prerogatives of certain of the sons of Esau corresponded to
the place and prerogatives of dukes.

Another point of evidence showing the desire of the English
translators to make the Scriptures better understood among
English-speaking people can be noted in the title often conferred
upon the owners of estates and plantations. These people are
called "lords," and this custom was very definitely not Hebraic.
No student of Hebrew religion and culture can conceive of
hearing an ancient Hebrew addressing a man by the same name
that he would give to his God. A man to the ancient Judaist was
a man-prophet, priest, king, Rabbi, Nazarite, miracle worker-
never "lord." This has to be a special adaptation so that feudal
England would be able to appreciate the position and power of
the man under the reference.

Unfortunate indeed has it been for black people in the
English-speaking world in particular, and in the western world
in general, that the King James translators did not employ in the
Bible text the term "Cush" or "Kush" or an English equivalent of
the Greek word "Ethiopia." If they had done so, then the English
Bible would present a clearer picture of the people involved.

Seventeenth century England was very familiar with the black
man from South Saharan Africa. The Greeks had been there; the
Romans had planted Christianity there; and the Muslims had
long since given the area a name meaning "blackman's land."

England, and in fact, Western Europe and the Mediterranean community, had seen him as slave and freedman for more than five hundred years. Sir John Hawkins,[4] who is known to have stood ashore at Alcatraz Island Off Cape Verde, shooting unsuspecting Africans in the distance for the fun of it, had entered the Atlantic slave trade in 1562; and such scholars must have been familiar with his coat of arms showing a helpless black man in chains. The English queen Elizabeth[5] and some prime businessmen had money invested in the trade and in the colonies to which they were being carried. By the year 1611, the black presence was part of the English and colonial scene but they were being called Negroes and not Ethiopians.

It could have been fear, or expediency, or a slave-trade mentality that constrained the King James translators to veil in obscurity the true identity of the people whom they called Ethiopians. The king and many captains of industry were involved in trade, and by 1611, England was competing with Portugal and Holland. She was also involved in colonizing in the New World, and English planters were using slave labor to produce the sugar and other crops that were on sale in Europe. It could have been these social and economic considerations that constrained the translators to resist the moral and spiritual obligation properly to identify the black folks about whom the Bible is speaking.

Looking back from this point in history, it is difficult to appreciate the claims of the King James translators that they "walked in ways of simplicity and integrity." They saw large landowners in ancient Hebrew history and called them "lords." They saw rulers of princedoms and called them "dukes." They saw those whom Europe called "Negroes" and they called them "Ethiopians," knowing full well that the common mind of England would not see that they were one and the same.

This term "Ethiopia" in the English Bible has mislead the Christian world for the past three-hundred-sixty-odd years, and it is highly conceivable that a more proper or an English term identification of the Cushites might have changed the whole European attitude towards chattel slavery for black people. The myths of savagery, cannibalism, and general debasement would have been reexamined had the Bible reflected the fact that the people under these myths were then being called "Negroes" in the Western world. The color and geography of the Cushites would have contributed to a better appreciation all around, and the most ignorant, rabid racist would not have pretended to doubt the existence of a soul in any man about whom he had read in the pages of the Holy Bible.

Ever since the Portuguese sailor-explorer, Vasco da Gama, rediscovered modern Ethiopia early in the sixteenth century, the Western world has known of the Christianity there and has made a definite distinction between the Ethiopian and the other sub-Saharan Africans. Providence in the form of inaccessibility and remoteness prevented the Muslims from destroying the Christianity in modern Ethiopia, but the fact that Christianity once flourished in Cush has not been made clear enough. To the white mind, the term "Ethiopian" has depicted a man who is definitely not a Negro. The Abyssinian's hair texture, skin color, and Arabian heritage has presented to the white world a white man in blackish color, and this is the image that has been brought to mind when the Bible mentions an Ethiopian. This is a false projection that has grown up and lasted because the self-professed "integrity" of the English translators was not strong enough to render a true and understandable identity of the black people about whom they were writing.

It is also sad to note that many of the twentieth century translators and revisionists still carry the term "Ethiopia" in the Bible text, and they should know that they are writing about a Sudanese area that was earlier known as Cush or Kush, and is so carried apparently in Hebrew texts.

The Revised Standard Version of the Bible was published in 1952, after having been voted as a project in 1951 by The National Council of The Churches of Christ in The U.S.A. The preface goes into considerable detail explaining the why of some of the changes that have been made. The body of explanations includes one that claims certain variances to have been necessary because time has changed the meaning of some of the words used in the King James Version, and that the old words no longer say what the King James scholars meant to say. While admitting that this is very keen thinking on the part of the Revised Standard revisionists, black understanding is very disappointed because the term "Ethiopia" is still used in the texts most of the time. A scanning of the entire edition shows the use of the word "Cush" in Genesis 2:13 and Ezekiel 38:5, and not having seen them we must allow for a few other such references, hoping that they will be found. Here again, in spite of a professed intention to improve and to clarify, the same old Ethiopian confusion is largely perpetuated.

Even now in 1974, there are millions of Bible readers who still think that the Ethiopia of the Bible is modern Ethiopia. This error lies uncorrected in the minds of millions of Bible readers and students—ministers, priests, nuns, deaconesses, church school teachers and seminarians. Across the entire world of Christian influence, people have no idea that the Holy Bible says anything pertaining to black Africa, in spite of the fact that the area of ancient Cush (Kush) lies almost due east of, and equally as southerly as Mauritania, which was the location of ancient Ghana that arose and flourished between 300 B.C. and 1200 A.D. And the area lies in the same relationship to ancient and modern Mali, whose King Mansa Musa and his kingdom appeared on European maps in 1372 with the inscription: "Mansa Musa, King of The Guinea Negroes, Richest King In Africa."[6]

The Greeks had identified the Cushites by their color, and the English equivalent would have been "black" or "Negro"-or the translators could have used Cush in the text instead of in the margin.

The question is, Would the Western world have visited such brutal and debasing treatment as it has done upon a people whom they knew were written about so favorably in Holy Writ? Beyond all doubt there would have been no question about whether or not they had souls, and there could have been no living myth that black Africa had been by-passed by civilization and was therefore wallowing in savagery and debasement.

The King James translators or someone went way ahead of history to put the name Greece in the mouth of the prophet Daniel,[7] and who can complain? The King James translators saw black Sudanese Africans in chains and called them "Negroes," but when they saw black Sudanese Africans sitting on the throne of Egypt they called them "Ethiopians," and literate England knew that people from the land that the people from the land that the Hebrews called Cush (or Kush) were victims of the slave trade. The Rev. Samuel Purchas wrote about them in 1610, and his statements are found in the book *Hakluytus Posthumus* or *Purchas His Pilgrimes*, Volume VI. His racial ideas are distorted, and his report on the attitude of the bereft families was in all likelihood given to him by men who sought to justify their trade, and therefore cannot be believed; yet the following quotation shows that he knew and that he told literate England who they were. In an Egyptian village which he called Hangia, Purchas claims to have seen what follows:

The merchants brought with them many Negroes; not the worst of their merchandise. These they buy of their parents, some thirty days journey above, and on the west side of the river (the Nile). As the wealth of others consists of multitudes of cattle (cattle), so theirs in the multitude of their children, whom they part from with as little passion; never after to be seene (seen) or heard of; regarding more the price then (than) condition of their slavery. These are descended of Chus (Cush or Kush), the sonne (son) of cursed Cham (Ham); as are all of that complexion. Not by reason of their seed, nor heat of the climate: nor of the soyle (soil), as some have supposed; for neither haply, will other races in that soyle (soil) proove black, nor that race in other soyles (soils) grow to better complexion: but rather from the curse of Noe (Noah) upon Cham (Ham) in the Posteritie of Chus (Cush or Kush).

The Rev. Samuel Purchas has left for himself a despicable legacy, because he knew that what he wrote about those unfortunate people was false. He knew that the Cushites were not accursed by anybody, and he also knew that Cush (or Kush) was a part of the Egyptian Empire for an aggregate total of over two thousand years. He knew that the people of Cush had put eighteen kings on the Egyptian throne, but the soul of Rev. Purchas had been destroyed by racism. The myths that went along with the slave trade had become far more important to him than the truths of the Bible. He was a Bible student, but he was also a slave to the color complex.

The King James translators could have protected subsequent generations from the color disease had they used the same term to designate the Cushite people of the Bible that England used to designate the Cushite people that they saw in chains. Modern Christian scholarship has inherited the solemn duty to clear away all the confusion at this point, for it exists until this day, and it obscures the historic truth that the Bible is ordained to teach.

Questions
1. What document brings modern Ethiopia into written history?
2. Why do modern Ethiopians claim not to be black people?
3. When did European powers recognize modern Ethiopia as the Kingdom of Abyssinia?
4. The Biblical term "Ethiopia" refers to what nation?
5. What is the literal meaning of the Greek term "Ethiopian"?
6. What is the modern name of the country that includes the land once known as Cush or Kush?
7. Why was the King James Version of the Bible translated?
8. Give the name and date of the first Englishman to enter the

Atlantic slave trade.

9. How many nations are mentioned by color in the English Bible?

10. Explain the relation between the people called "Ethiopians" in the King James Bible and those called "Negroes" by Europe in 1611.

Notes

1. The Grolier Society, *Lands and People*, Vol. 5 (Toronto-New York: The Grolier Society, 1929). Other sources give the same information.

2. *Encyclopedia Americana*, 1953 ed.

3. *Ibid.* However, Russell Warren Howe, in *Black Africa*, p.21, says "To the Arabs, all countries south of the Northern Desert were Bilad as-Sudan. . . ."

4. James Pope Hennessy, *Sins of the Fathers* (Alfred A. Knopf, New York, 1967), p. 51.

5. Basil Davidson, *The Black Mother* (Boston-Toronto: Little, Brown, 1961),

6. Several authors report this story, among them are Basil Davidson and Margaret Shinnie.

7. Daniel 11:2, refers to Grecia.

3

THE COLOR OF THE EGYPTIANS

Chronological History of Egypt

Herodotus (speaking from a survey of Egyptian records) 450 B.C.; "Thus the whole number years is 11,340."

Derivation:	Belongs to the Sahara-Sudanese region and culture.
12,000 B.C.	The land upon which Egypt stands begins to emerge, built up by silt deposited from the Nile River.
10,000 B.C.	Stone work from excavations shows Nubia and Upper Egypt (southern) to have been the most progressive area in the world.[1]
9,000–8,000 B.C.	Egypt's land becomes habitable: Emergence of The Tasian culture, the earliest recognized farmers.
6,000–5,000 B.C.	The Nile Valley has become a population center.
5,000 B.C.	(as early as) Becomes detached from the general African context.

4,500–3,200 B.C.	Rise of pre-dynastic Egypt, of which little is known.
4,241 B.C.	The Egyptian calendar and hieroglyphic writing appear.
4,000 B.C.	The Badarian culture has succeeded the Tasian; a more vigorous group said to have had tropical physical features called "negroid features." Used sundried brick.
3,400 B.C.	Two Nile Valley kingdoms are mature, the upper (southern Egypt) and the lower (northern Egypt); there are cities, etc.
3,400–3,200 B.C.	Begins old kingdom, ruled by Min (Menes) or Narmer, first king to use title Pharaoh: southern kingdom has conquered the northern kingdom.
2,000 or 2600 B.C.	Great pyramid at Gizeh: ordered built by Cheops.
2,650–2,480 B.C.	The Sixth Dynasty; expeditions sent down the Red Sea and into the southwest.
2,475 B.C.	The fall of the old kingdom.
2,340 B.C.	Begins Sixth Dynasty; expeditions perhaps went to the fringes of the Congo.
2,200 B.C.	An Asian raid, plus a revolution, brings the first intermediate period of confusion and reorganization; centralized authority gave way to one rule by powerful feudal nobles.
2,130 B.C.	Begins middle kingdom; Eleventh Dynasty brings peace; rise of the middle class; power has shifted from Memphis to Thebes. *Note: Egypt conquers all Nubia—Cush, Wawat, Irthet; kingdom extends into the Sudan to distance of one hundred miles of modern Khartoum.*
1780 B.C.	The Hyksos Asians (shepherd kings) conquer and rule Egypt—said to have been the Hittites, but actually an unknown people; second intermediate period ends; Kush regains independence.
1715 B.C.	Joseph the Hebrew becomes governor of Egypt under the Hyksos Tyrant.

1706 B.C.	Jacob moves the family to Egypt.
1580 B.C.	"Now there arose up a new king over Egypt, which knew not Joseph" (Exod. 1:8); begins Eighteenth Dynasty; Hyksos driven back into Asia (maybe Palestine) by Amenophis of Thebes. *Note: Thutmosis I reconquered Kush and went probably as far as Khartoum.*
1371 B.C.	The birth of Moses.
1225 B.C. (circa)	It is sometimes concluded that the Exodus took place during the reign of Thutmosis III or of Meremptah.
1150 B.C.	Collapse of the New Kingdom.
1000 B.C.	Egyptian power is in decline; Pinhasi is governor of Cush. During this period Solomon marries Pharaoh's daughter.
945 B.C.	Shishak (Bible spelling) or Sheshonk I begins Twenty-second Dynasty; the first Libyan pharaoh; raided Judah 923 B.C. and put it to tribute—claimed to have captured 133 towns and cities.
751 B.C.	Kashta the Cushite begins the Twenty-fifth Dynasty; Cushite kings held power for one hundred fifty years: Piankhy (751–716); Shabako (716–685?); Shabataka (701–690); Taharqua (biblical Tirhakah) (690–664); Tanutaman (664–656).
660 B.C.	Assyrians invaded Egypt and dethroned Tanutaman; introduced iron weapons; did not colonize Egypt.
525 B.C.	Persians conquer Egypt led by Cambyses; invaded Cush also—Judah and parts of Cush are parts of the same empire.
332 B.C.	Alexander the Great of Greece conquered Egypt and Persia.
30 B.C.	Rome conquered Egypt. There was no conqueror in Egypt during the Barbarian conquest of the Roman Empire.
640 A.D.	Arab Muslims conquer and settle in Egypt.
1798 A.D.	The French conquer Egypt.

1801 A.D.	The British force the French to withdraw from Egypt.
1805–1822 A.D.	Mohamet Ali, also rules Nubia and the Sudan.
1879 A.D.	Ismail Pasha abdicated.
1822 A.D.	The British occupied Egypt.
1914 A.D.	Britain proclaimed Egypt to be a protectorate.
1922 A.D.	Faud I reestablished the kingdom which was changed under Farouk I, 1936.
1945	The Arab League is in power.

UNTIL VERY RECENTLY, most of the historians and writers have conveyed to the world the idea that the earliest Egyptians were white, or at least near-white, and any blackness found among them was imported with slavery. This is never quite spoken outright, but it has been often conveyed in the kind of emphasis laid upon the racial mixture of early Egypt; in addition, the idea occurs in almost all attempts to depict the scenes through visual representation.

The subtlety of portraying white over black in ancient Egypt finds a most ingenious example in a compact little book called *From Ur to Rome*, which was written for high school children by K.M. Gadd.[2] Chapter Ten begins under the caption "Every Day Life In Egypt," and relates that most of the poorer people worked on the land and in the personal service of the king, the nobles, and the priests; and it says, "often they were slaves." On page 73, there is a sketch, presumably a copy of Egyptian paintings, showing workmen and slaves at their tasks. All the people portrayed as workmen are dark brown and black; but when one turns to page 75, there is a sketch portraying apparently young nobility at play, and each person is shown to be white! Nothing is said about the color of the people, but the pictures reveal both the author's mind and intention.

Another prime example of subtle racism in dealing with early Egypt is found in *History of Europe—Ancient and Medieval* by

Robinson and Breasted;[3] it is indicated that Chapter Two—"The Story of Egypt," was written by Breasted. On page 14, he speaks of the Egypt of today (1929), and describes the irrigation canal workers as "Brown skinned men of slender build, with dark hair." On page 16, while dealing with the earliest Nile dweller, he points out that the valley peasant labored likewise six thousand years ago. He does not say that the earlier ones were "brown-skinned," but he also does not pause to say that the color scheme has been diluted by twelve hundred years and over a half-dozen invasions that included Arab settlement and colonization around 700 A.D.

But worse yet is the fact that an inside cover page contains what is labeled a "Portrait Bust of Queen Norfretete, wife of Ikhnaton and mother-in-law of Tutenkhamon. Fourteenth century B.C. (after Ludwig Borchardt)"; in the picture, Queen Norfretete is whiter than Queen Elizabeth! She is shown to be pure Aryan or Nordic. Hence, the book shows the reader what to think without telling him outright, and it teaches him to conceive of Queen Norfretete (or Nertertari or Nefertiti) as having been a white woman; and this is in spite of the fact that she is known to have been black and very beautiful.

A modern illustration of the historic confusion concerning the color of the ancient Egyptian comes from a source which ordinarily puts forth efforts to destroy racial myths. This refers to Margaret Shinnie who writes: "In their wall paintings, the Egyptians showed the Kushites as having dark skins in contrast to their own lighter ones, and sometimes drew their hair differently."[4]

The difficulty here lies not in the report that the paintings show different colors, but the phrase "having dark skins in contrast to their own lighter ones" conveys an idea which she most likely did not intend to convey. The term "contrast" suggests extremes—unlikeness, a condition that cannot be applied to the ancient Egyptian color scheme. In looking at the paintings, she could only see a variation in coloredness—a lighter-than-dark skin, but not enough difference to form a contrast.

Many of the present day historians bring us closer to the truth about the color of ancient Egyptians. Paul Bohannon holds that Egypt was basically an African culture with intrusions of Asian culture.

Basil Davidson, one of the world's most knowledgeable African historian, believes that the ancient Egyptians "belonged . . . not to any specific Egyptian region or Near Eastern heritage, but to that wide community of peoples who lived between the Red Sea and the Atlantic Ocean, shared a common 'Saharan—Sudanese' culture; and drew their reinforcements from the same source; even though, as time went by, they also absorbed a number of wanderers from the Near East."

Davidson further says, "It is similarly clear that the familiar attribution of the term 'white' to the North African and Nile Valley stocks (as of the term 'black' to the others) is merely a latter mystification of the racial sort. Those old Cro-Magnon Europeans and Caucasoids who came into North Africa some 12,000 years ago were quite surely far from blonde, and any notion that they were European in the modern sense can be safely dismissed."[5]

E. Jefferson Murphy discourages anyone who seeks to determine the race of people now extinct by the study of fossil and measurements of same. Says he, "There are too many other genetic factors involved (hair, skin, blood type) for one to describe an individual's race by his skeletal characteristics after several thousand years have passed. Race is, after all, basically a statistical abstraction, derived by measuring dozens of traits of a population, then using averages, medians, norms, and other statistical (and arbitrary) points to formulate a description; the individual rarely possesses all the traits of his race."[6]

He joins the school of historians who find that the ancient Egyptians were fundamentally an African people that were racially mixed and with fewer so called "negroid" genes than their Nubian neighbors. As do others, Murphy knows that the Badarians of approximately 4000 B.C. have left a profusion of skeletal remains that show these so called "negroid" traits.

Lerone Bennett finds that the "Badarian culture proves that black men camped on the banks of the Nile thousands of years before the Egypt of Pharaohs," and further reports that "bodies were excavated at El Badari amid artifacts suggesting a date of about 8000 B.C." He further states that the evidence suggests that ancient Egyptians were "black-, brown- and yellow-skinned people who sprang from a mixture of Negro, Semitic and Caucasian stocks," and painted themselves in black, reddish brown and yellow.[7]

Every high school student in the United States should be made familiar with the eyewitness description of the color of the ancient Egyptians that is inferred by the man who is called the "The Father of History." The man's name is Herodotus, the Greek historian who visited Egypt approximately four hundred fifty years before Christ was born. In his *Second Book, Entitled Euterpe* he writes about a group of people which he calls "the Colchians," who can even now be traced to that portion of present-day Russia that is called the Georgian Soviet Socialist Republic, the area in which the dark-appearing Joseph Stalin was born. Herodotus believed beyond doubt that these Colchians (modern Georgians) were an Egyptian race, possibly descendants of an Egyptian army led there by the famed conqueror Sisostris. He based his conclusion upon several factors, and the first-named factor was their color. He said of the Colchians, "They are black-skinned and have wooly hair." This was not his strongest reason he said, because he had seen "several other nations" with these characteristics.

One scholar can argue with another about conclusions based upon written documents, or upon the study of fossils and artifacts, or upon expressed opinions, modern or ancient; but no scholar that was born later than 450 B.C. can argue with Herodotus about that which he saw with his natural eyes. No matter how unscientific or inadequate may be a scholar's approach to history, no one except another eyewitness can tell him whether an object is white or black when he is looking at it; and since Herodotus concluded that the black skin and wooly hair of the Colchians at whom he looked was a fact to help prove their descendancy from Egyptians, then he is saying that his eyes had found the Egyptians to be "black-skinned with wooly hair." He does not describe the degree of their blackness, nor does he describe the length of their hair, nor the size of noses or lips. These features were of no importance to Herodotus, and should be of no importance today.

It must always be kept in mind that all things pertaining to Egypt changed very slowly, as was the case throughout the ancient world. Drastic changes were only wrought by invasions and colonization, and in the case of Egypt the Hyksos tyrants had long been driven from the land, and the Assyrian victors had withdrawn without colonizing. The Babylonians and Persians had brought only their armies, and the Greeks, Romans, and Arabs had not come. Therefore, the basic color scheme that was beheld by Herodotus was undoubtedly the same that was beheld by Abraham and Jacob and Joseph. In truth, the lighter-skinned Hyksos conquerors were there to welcome Abraham and Jacob, but the population had only been diluted by immigrants from Libya and the Sudan very largely.

As intelligent as he was, it is positively unthinkable that Herodotus would have made an extended visit to a land of people visibly of different colors, and then have mistakenly inferred that they had black skins; it must therefore be assumed that whatever mixture there was still represented some shades of black in his eyes. Those paintings that have been found to represent people who were obviously too light to be called black could possibly have been left by the Hyksos culture that rode astride Egyptian culture for two hundred years.

Many scholars base their idea of a multicolored ancient Egyptian population partially upon a study of the language. The language has been judged to have been Semitic, and this in their minds means that a strong Asian influence was there. However, since the Egyptian tongue was the oldest of record, it might someday be determined that the Semites spoke a form of the African of which Egyptian was an adaptation. Egypt was definitely not a borrower from her neighbors. The Mediterranean world had little to lend or give to Egypt. Hers was the mother civilization that helped to give birth to others, and it is possible that language was a gift from Egypt.

A final argument needs merely to introduce the question, "To what do people migrate? We know that people do not nor did they ever migrate to nothingness. People who cross boundaries of wilderness, deserts, and seas to take up permanent residence yonder are assured of subsistence and security; and these can only be assured if people are already there. As the Nile built up the land of Egypt, people came into it no doubt from the south, and later migrants found them there.

Any concessions that we make to the historic theory of a multicolored Egypt are not conclusively demanded by the facts at hand, and when we make such concessions we can safely go no further than a quotation taken from the works of Lerone Bennett:[8] "Great Negro scholars (W.E.B. DuBois, Carter G. Woodson, William Leo Hansberry) have insisted that the ancient Egyptians, from Menes to Cleopatra, were a mixed race which presented the same physical types and color ranges as American Negroes—a people, in short, who would have been forced to sit on the back seats of the busses of Mississippi." Bennett then quotes Carter G. Woodson as having said, "If the Egyptians and the majority of the tribes of northern Africa were not Negroes, then there are no Negroes in the United States."

The Egyptians of Old Testament times were overwhelmingly a black-skinned people. The story of Joseph opens upon a black-skinned nation who had lost their freedom and their country because of an Asian invasion, but dating from the beginning of her years of oppression there, Israel shared community with a black-skinned people who were masters of their land. Blackness in the eyes of the children of Israel was a natural color to see, a natural color to live with, a natural color to be. Later chapters will show that Israel's nationhood was built up out of these people.

Questions
1. From what culture did ancient Egypt derive?
2. How did the land called Egypt come to be?
3. When did the land of Egypt become habitable?
4. When did Egypt first annex the country of Cush?
5. What kings ruled Egypt when Abraham went there? When Joseph was taken there? When Jacob migrated there?
6. Name the king that began the Cushite dynasty of Egypt.
7. How does Herodotus connote that ancient Egyptians were black?
8. Were the ancient Egyptians fundamentally an Asian or African people?
9. To what do people migrate?
10. Why would ancient Egyptians feel at home in today's Harlem of New York City?

Notes
1. This and most other facts about ancient Egypt are widely reported by historians.
2. K.M. Gadd, *From Ur to Rome* (London: Ginn, 1936).
3. Breasted and Robinson, *History of Europe—Ancient and Medieval* (New York, London: Ginn, 1929).
4. Ancient African Kingdoms.
5. Ibid.
6. *History of African Civilizations,* by E. Jefferson Murphy. Seligman also attempts to discuss the races of Africa in his book by that name but he concedes that for descriptive purposes one cannot say much more than that which we find in A.C. Haddon's definition of race: "a group of peoples who have certain well marked physical

characters in common."

7. Lerone Bennett, Jr., *Before the Mayflower* (Baltimore: Penguin Books, 1962), p. 7.
8. *Ibid.*

4

THE LAND OF CUSH

THERE HAVE BEEN VERY FEW nations or peoples in world history who accomplished as much in their day, and yet are so little known today as the people of Cush. Their glorious history is such that they should be known to every high school student of today, and as yet few students or former students know anything about them whatsoever. A great many of the facts in this chapter will be reiterated in Chapter 9.

At various times during their long and exciting history, they built the then world's biggest iron foundry and sent its products into many parts of the earth. As an overrun and an annexed people, they still became strong enough to dominate their conquerors and take possession of the greatest throne on earth at the time. They sent their merchant ships into the ports of the Mediterranean world, and also bought and sold merchandise in the ports of the Red Sea and the Indian Ocean. Their merchant seamen were familiar sights in ancient Jerusalem, as well as in seaport trading centers of India and China. Their warrior kings led military expeditions into areas in North Africa and Asia, conquering Syria and Judah. Their fame as a great nation was so widely known that the Psalmist of Israel acknowledged the prestige in being able to say that "this or that man was born there." Before the fourth century B.C., Cush was one of the best-known nations in the Old Testament world.

When historians call Cush the oldest purely African kingdom in history to become a world power, they are speaking of it in contrast to the idea that Asiatic and Mediterranean people played a vital part in the development of ancient Egypt; rightly so, for the history of Cush reveals no appreciable amount of non-African migrations at any point in its history.

The Cushites, who are sometimes called Kushites by different writers, were the earliest inhabitants of the vast land area lying around the upper Nile between Egypt and Abyssinia, the latter of which is called Ethiopia today. The area under discussion corresponds to the modern nation of Sudan—an area which was named Nubia by the Christians. Apparently the name might have been given to the area by Egypt; in any case, it appears as such in Egyptian records as early as 2000 B.C. Their territory extended from above the third cataract of the Nile River to perhaps the sixth cataract. It has been rather definitely determined that the southern boundary of Cush reached a point approximately one hundred miles from the modern city of Khartoum.

These Cushites were among the world's earliest farmers, and they were some of the first farmers among the people of the Nile Valley. The kingdom is said to have been greatly enlarged around 3000 B.C. because of the steady and awful desiccation of the once green and verdant Sahara area. When its inhabitants pushed their way in several directions to escape the famine that accompanied the drying up of what is now the Sahara Desert, many of them found a new home in the area of Cush, whose agriculture continued to depend upon the Nile River.

Anthropologists and scholars in other fields of science have discovered proof that the Sahara became habitable sometime after

10,000 B.C., and the land there became fertile, made so by flowing rivers. Verdancy in the Sahara reached its peak during the Makalian or "wet phase" that occurred reportedly between about 5500 or 2500 B.C. Its inhabitants were fishers, hunters, herdsmen and farmers, and as they left the drying Sahara, they carried some of their culture and techniques into Cush and several other areas south and north. The last fifty years have seen a tremendous increase in the study and knowledge of Cush, and we are told to expect more and more information to continue to flow from continuing investigations.

Its civilization was closely akin to that of predynastic Egypt, and during an early stage, prior to about 5000 B.C., was more progressive. It could have been that the migrations from the Sahara helped to make it so. At first the Egyptian hieroglyphics formed the script of Cush, but at some point during the third century, these ingenious people invented a script of their own, although the Egyptian hieroglyphics continued in use in the temple worship. Incidentally, the Cushite script has never been translated.

From the results of various excavations, we now know some of the things that were used in ancient Cush. The finds have given evidence of the use of jewelry, pottery, glass, metalware, tools, and weapons. Remnants of houses have been unearthed, as well as carvings and paintings. They built temples of worship, and for their kings and queens they often built pyramids which were smaller and different in shape from those of Egypt.

Many Cushites were metalworkers who used bronze, copper, silver, and gold. It was noted in ancient times that there was gold in abundance in Cush. Royal gravesites have yielded necklaces, rings, earrings and bracelets. For these people it is said that bronze was the rarest metal.

In their houses were found grindstones, pottery, baskets, and "simple tools of stone, such as arrowheads for hunting, or metal knives, axeheads, swords, and razors."[1] In other instances there were probably imported wares such as glass bottles and vases, bowls, and other vessels from later Egypt and even from the Romans much later. The pottery of Meroe, the greatest city and last capital of Cush, has left samples of kitchenware, cooking vessels, beer pots, bowls and basins; much of the pottery was painted with paint derived from the earth and from other sources. Herodotus is actually the ancient who noted that Cush had gold in abundance, and he added that there one found huge elephants, ebony, and all sorts of wild trees.

The development of Cushite civilization is historically divided into two phases. The earliest phase of its development centered around Napata, its first capital. The latter and more expansive phase centered around the later capital, the city of Meroe; this is sometimes called the Birmingham of Africa because of its huge foundry works. Basil Davidson gives an accurate summary of the present-day historian's estimate of the Cushite civilization emanating from Meroe:

> Meroe became very much a civilization in its own right; and this civilization was one of considerable depth and range of culture. The history of Meroitic Cush covers at least six centuries of energetic and often quite distinctive development in many fields, especially those of Town and Temple building, metal manufacture and the elaboration of international trade with countries as remote as India and China.[2]

It is Meroitic Cush that is frequently mentioned in the writings of the Hebrew prophets as will be shown in chapters 5, 8, 9 and 10.

E. Jefferson Murphy[3] believes that the growth and expansion of Meroe were based upon certain natural advantages that were found in lesser degree, if at all, around Napata. For example, Mero had a more sufficient rainfall to support the profuse growth of grass and trees, and of course, the great iron industry there could not have been possible had it not been endowed with iron ore deposits.

Meroe's location itself was highly advantageous, for it was located in a small triangle between the Nile and Atbara rivers. Actually, it was set astride the growing trade between interior Africa and the trading ports of the Red Sea and Indian Ocean. In a few weeks the caravans could travel from Mero to the Red Sea, and from thence goods went back and forth to Arabia, India, Persia, Rome, and Greece. There might even have been boat and barge traffic up and down the Nile, for the Holy Bible, as will be seen later, mentions the ships made of bullrushes.

Dynastic Egypt began its intrusion into Cush during the reign of Amenophis, whose dates are 1991–1962 B.C., but the actual conquest was consummated during the time of the great warrior king, Sisostris. He went beyond the land boundaries of Cush and, according to his own belief, reached "the end of the earth."

Egypt was able to pacify Cush under its domination, and it became an integral part of the empire. Cush itself largely accepted its place in the empire for the time, but it never really and thoroughly absorbed Egyptian culture. Their own type and distinctive civilization continued to develop.

As was shown in the chronology of the preceding chapter, the land of Cush was not a part of Egypt proper during the earliest days of the sojourn of the Children of Israel, because the conquest of the Hyksos shepherd kings gave opportunity for Cush to regain its independence. But the two hundred years of Cushite independence were terminated when the Egyptians succeeded in driving out the Hyksos tyrants, and this happened during the latter part of Israel's sojourn in Egypt. The famed Thutmosis I drove his army all the way to modern Khartoum.

It was about 700 B.C. when the Cushite kings became strong enough to seize the most powerful throne in their world. This feat was accomplished by King Kashta, and the overthrown pharaoh was a Libyan. Kashta began Egypt's Twenty-fifth Dynasty, and extended his rule all the way to Thebes; but it was his son Piankhy and his grandson Tahakaka (or Tirhakah), an ally of Judah (see Chapter 9), who cut the widest swathes on the battlefields of their day.

Piankhy was unable to restore Egypt to its former glory, but he tried. He ruled a fourth the African continent, and his kingdom stretched from the shores of the Mediterranean Sea to the borders of modern-day Ethiopia. John Hope Franklin, in describing the exploits of Piankhy, says this: "With his large contingent of trained soldiers and river Navy he routed the Libyans who were threatening his position in the area below Thebes. One by one the cities of the northern region, Heracheopolis, Memphis, Heliopolis, Mesed, fell before the might of this wily Ethiopian. When Piankhy returned to his capital, Napata, he had subdued sixteen Princes and had made Egypt a dependency of Cush."[4] A Greek historian said that the Cushites bound their prisoners with gold chains and used weapons tipped with stone.

Piankhy's son, the Biblical Tirhakah (Taharga), ruled from the city of Tanis, and is acclaimed as the most outstanding of the Cushite pharaohs of the Twenty-fifth Dynasty; he was certainly its greatest conqueror. He ascended to the throne during the forty-second year of his life, in or about 690 or 683 B.C., and his ascension coincided with a tremendous Nile flood, which he regarded as a good omen of his reign. Said he: "Moreover the sky rained in Nubia, it made all the hills glisten. Every man had abundance of everything, Egypt was in happy festival."

Lerone Bennett shares with us a statement made by Sir E.A. Wallis Budge. He was of Tirhakah: "His deeds appealed so strongly to the popular imagination, at all events in Greek times, that they were regarded as the exploits of a hero." Chapter 9 gives a more complete record of Tirhakah.

When forced to forsake Egypt, the Cushite leaders returned to their homeland not to die, but to live and grow and glow, for its highest attainments came to pass after their return. The population of Cush had not followed the army into Egypt. There had been no wholesale exodus of Cushites to the north, so their civilization could continue to develop without serious disruption. It could have been the Persian invasion of Cush in 591 B.C. that caused the kings to move the capital to Meroe, and in re-adopting their own culture they worshipped the God Apedemak, who was later depicted in full face rather than in profile, and having multiple heads and arms. Cushite civilization reached its peak about 250 B.C. and 150 A.D. Its power and culture spread over an area of nearly one thousand miles up and down the Nile.

Cush died under the invasion of the Axumites, who were the forerunners of modern Ethiopia, also known as Abyssinia. The Axumites were led by the warrior king Ezana, and Meroe was sacked in 325 of the Christian Era; in the years following its downfall, a number of independent kingdoms continued to exist. The new kingdoms were referred to as the Noba and the Red Noba (Nubians), the last of the people who left the dry Sahara lands and settled in the Nile Valley. The largest and most northerly of the post-Cushite kingdoms was Nobatia. In the center was the kingdom of Makuria, and the most southerly kingdom was Alwa.

In 540 A.D., the Emperor Justinian and his wife Theodora sent Julian, the sainted missionary, on a mission to Nubia; and, as he did in Abyssinia, he met with great success in bringing Christianity to the area. Both Julian and his successor Longinus spent many fruitful years in converting the Nubians to the faith. These Christians were very faithful and formed close ties with Christian Alexandria and also with the Coptic Church of modern Ethiopia. It is pointed out that Strabo the Roman mentioned Cush in his writings.

The Cushites attacked a Roman garrison in Syene sometime near 25 A.D., and carried way a statue of Emperor Augustus. They were thereafter conquered by Gaius Petronus. They sought peace through an ambassador sent to the Roman emperor while at Sames, but a Greek papyrus mentions a skirmish in the desert between the Romans and the Cushites as late as 64 A.D. The Cushites also saw Nero, for he passed through and went to a point south of Meroe.

By the opening of the seventh century A.D., most of the Nubians had become Christians, and used Greek, Coptic and Nubian languages in their church liturgies. Learning was encouraged, and a great program of building monasteries and churches was begun. Christian activity must have been very much in evidence around the capitals, Dongola in the north and Soba in the south.

We can only wonder what would have happened to Nubia had it been left to develop under Christian faith; but alas it was not, for in 643 A.D. Egypt was overrun by Muslim Arabs, and Nubia was almost cut off completely from the rest of the Christian world. Davidson says, "For 600 years its kings and bishops, contemporaries of the kings and bishops building the Holy Roman Empire in Europe, were practically unknown to that empire, and had only themselves to rely on for faith and assurance."

The fatimid sect of Muslim rulers apparently suffered the continued existence of Christianity in Nubia, just as it had tolerated the Coptic Christians in Egypt. But they were ousted from power in the twelfth century by the Saracens who invaded Egypt from Syria under the leadership of Saladin, made famous in history by the crusades which were then going on. In 1317, the king of Nobatia was a Muslim puppet, and Christianity soon disappeared there. Alwa lived on as a Christian kingdom until invaded by the Funj Sect of Muslims from the north and west early in the sixteenth century. The kingdom of Soba was permanently destroyed in 1504. The Funj people intermarried with the indigenous Nubians, and Christianity ceased to exist. Thus nine hundred years after the earliest Christian missionaries had reached Nubia, Christian days came to an end. The people remained virtually isolated from the Christian world until the coming of the European explorers and missionaries that helped pave the way for European colonialism.

The death of Nubian Christianity reminds us of a similar

tragedy that occurred many miles away in West Africa, but not so far away in time.

The Portuguese planted Christianity in Benin in 1470 and in the kingdom of Kongo (in present-day Angola) in 1482. The Mwani Congo, ruler of the latter-named kingdom, paid the salaries of Christian missionaries sent from Portugal to his kingdom to teach and spread Christian faith. The king's nephew and son were sent to Portugal to study, and the son went from Portugal to study for the priesthood at the Vatican. The king of Kongo was himself a baptized Christian by 1506, and his son the priest was elevated to the Roman Catholic Bishopric in 1518. Here again African Christianity died out, but this time its death was caused by the Atlantic slave trade and not the Muslim invasion.

Today, Meroe is in worse condition than the ancient thriving city of Timbuctu, for the latter is yet a poor little village. But Meroe is uninhabited, having long rows of crumbling pyramids, and great mounds of earth covering the slag heaps, the palaces, and the dwellings. The ruins of other Meroitic towns run for some miles to the east between the Nile and Atbara rivers.

Questions

1. What was the oldest inner-African kingdom to become a world power?
2. Give the approximate boundaries of ancient Cush.
3. Did the Cushites build pyramids?
4. What historian first mentions the gold, elephants and ebony of Cush?
5. Name the first capital of Cush?
6. Name the second capital of Cush.
7. Why is the second capital of Cush called "the Birmingham of Africa"?
8. Can you give the approximate date that Cushite kings gained the throne of Egypt?
9. Can you remember anything about Piankhy?

10. Who carried Christianity into Cush? In what year?
11. By whom was Cushite Christianity obliterated?
12. What is the literal translation of the Arabic word "Sudan"?

Notes

1. *Ibid.*
2. This is another set of facts generally reported by historians.
3. *Ibid.*
4. John H. Franklin, *From Slavery to Freedom* (New York: Alfred A. Knopf, 1947).

5

THE OLD TESTAMENT WORLD REGARD FOR BLACK PEOPLE

AFTER THE ELAPSE OF several generations, an oppressed people lose the psychological self-regard derived from a latent memory of what they once were; that is unless the written or oral history of their pre-oppression forebears is constantly rehearsed in their ears as children. Meanwhile, an oppressor would never by word or deed say to his victims that their forebears knew a day of greatness before some stronger tyrant managed to subject them. This would be an acknowledgement on the part of the oppressor that the situation is unnatural, and was brought about by his own ability for rapine. So the oppressor must encourage the downtrodden to feel that his condition is the result of an innate flaw or debasement, usually something that has been his undoing from the beginning of his kind.

This is the kind of attitude that Israel showed towards the Canaanites. The Canaanites did not lose their land because the Hebrews coveted it and shed oceans of Canaanite blood to get it. The Canaanites, said Israel, lost their land and their freedom because of their innately abominable way of life, which so offended God that forgiveness and correction were impossible. In order to live with them, these people had to be subdued, subjected, oppressed, and forever barred from the Temple.

This type of propaganda becomes very effective when there is no history around to remind them of former days of greatness. They will be inclined to accept for themselves the attitude of the oppressor, even though the strong-minded person among them will feel that his own personal potentialities have overcome the primitive past. He will feel that at some point in time the innate malignancy has been healed, and he will call upon his brethren to dedicate themselves to the task of lifting their people to the heights that the oppressor has known forever.

This lack of knowledge and proper understanding of their history has placed a psychological burden upon the black Americans. Many of them are exposed to a little bit of their history, but the exposure comes after childhood has passed and the damage has already been done; because by then they may not be quite sure that such greatness was ever really there, and if did exist, they are not quite certain of their relationship to it.

If someone should ask the average black Christian today what the Holy Bible has to say about black people, at least two passages would likely come to mind. It is likely that all those who grew up with Sunday schools and church-related activities have heard over and over the two passages to be discussed.

In the Prophecy of Jeremiah (13:23) a question is asked that has become one of the most familiar Bible passages: "Can the Ethiopian change his skin, or the leopard his spots?" Everybody readily understands this to mean that as God made something or someone, so it or he will continue to be; but the racial propaganda situation in America has added a somber psychological note

that Jeremiah certainly did not intend. For example, this statement would just never be employed to say that Moses could
never have been other than what he was, or that Jesus Christ,
because of the uplifted nature of being, could never change and
be different. The passage from Jeremiah is almost always used to
say that one must be content with the misfortune of being what
he is, for into the American mind comes the picture of the poor
unfortunate Ethiopian who would most certainly change his skin
if he could; but alas he cannot. Here is the picture of a man who
would be something better if he could. This psychosis runs the
gamut between both extremes of racial bigotry. The ranting racist
will say to his audience, "You Liberals may say what you will,
but the Bible says that the Ethiopian (he will say 'Nigger') cannot
change his skin, nor the leopard his spots." While at the other
extreme the benign Sunday school teacher might say to her class,
"Children, do not hate people because of their color. Remember,
the Bible teaches us that the Ethiopian (she will say 'little colored
boy') cannot change his skin, nor the leopard his spots."

Jeremiah was not commiserating either with the Ethiopian or
the leopard. (And, incidentally, even the rabid racist does not feel
that among animals there is anything unfortunate in the fact that
leopards have spots.) Jeremiah knew that the Ethiopian's land
was bigger than his own, more powerful than his own, and
richer than his own. He also knew, as will be shown later, that
his people at that very moment were overly dependent upon
these Ethiopians. Furthermore, he knew that the Ethiopian was
proud of his skin and would not have changed it if he could.
Jeremiah also knew that his psalm-writing countryman had
acknowledged that Ethiopia was a great place in which to be
born.[1]

Jeremiah was a man who used colorful speech, and in this as
in other instances, he used a man and an animal that would
make his analogy graphic and vivid. The lesson that he wanted
to teach is the next clause: "Then May Ye also do Good, that are
accustomed to evil." It is reasonable to say that Jeremiah might

have asked if the white man can change his skin, if there had been any around in Jeremiah's day, but there were not.

Another passage that is widely familiar and often misconstrued is the reference of Psalm 68:31. The second clause of the sentence says, "Ethiopia shall soon stretch out Her Hands unto God." This has been a favorite passage for some of the orators of the past. They have pictured an enslaved, down-trodden Ethiopia, feebly, but faithfully, stretching forth her hands to God; praying for the day when God would lift their bondage.

Many people have never taken the time to read that the Psalm praises "Jah," the God that "rideth upon the Heavens," and who brought Israel out of bondage. He will continue to enlarge Israel's fortunes, because Israel is faithful to Him. Because they have built the Temple, says the twenty-ninth verse, kings will be converted and bring offerings thereto. Great and strong warrior nations will be severely dealt with so that "Princes shall come out of Egypt; Ethiopia shall soon stretch out her hands unto God." In spite of all their might and power, Egypt and Ethiopia would not be too great for God to bring unto Himself upon their knees. The psalmist points to a great and powerful nation, and not to one that is already downtrodden.

In the remainder of this chapter we shall take an overall view of the question of how black people were regarded in the Old Testament world; the following quotation from Lerone Bennett sets the tone:[2]

> Back there, in the beginning, blackness was not an occasion for obloquy. In fact, the reverse seems to have been true. White men were sometimes ridiculed for the unnatural whiteness of their skin. . . . Black people were known and honored throughout the ancient world. Ancient Ethiopia, a vaguely defined territory somewhere to the South of Egypt, was hailed as a place fit for the vacations of the Gods, Homer praised Memmon, King of Ethiopia, and black Eurybates:

"Of visage solemn, sad, but sable hue,
Short, wooly curls, o'er fleeced his bending
head, . . .
Eurybates, in whose large soul alone,
Ulysses viewed an image of his own."

Bennett further tells us that Homer, Herodotus, Pliny, Diodorus and other classical writers praised the Ethiopians, and he also offers the following quotation from the works of Lady Flora Louise Lugard:

The Annals of all the great early nations of Asia Minor are full of them. The Mosaic (biblical) records allude to them frequently; but while they are described as the most powerful, the most just, and the most beautiful of the human race, they are constantly spoken of as black, and there seems to be no other conclusion to be drawn, than that at that remote period of history the leading race of the Western World was a black race.

Finally from Bennett's work comes a statement written by the Greek historian Diodorus Siculus in the first century B.C. "The Ethiopians conceived themselves to be of greater antiquity than any other nation; and it is probable that, born under the sun's path, its warmth may have ripened them earlier than other men." (The propaganda that says the black man was by-passed by civilization certainly did not come from this Grecian).

Basil Davidson[3] says that the ancient Greeks wrote that it was to the land of the "blameless Ethiopians" that Homer's gods repaired once a year to feast for twelve days. He could have added also that Homeric heroes such as Memelaus, King of Sparta (or Lacedaemon) included Ethiopia in his travels.

Herodotus in his *Histories* seems to have written more about the Ethiopians than other Greek writers, and he more than pre-echoes the modern Afro-American sentiment that "Black is beautiful." Says Herodotus: "Where the south declines towards the setting sun lies the country called Ethiopia, that last inhabited land in that direction. There gold is obtained in great plenty, huge elephants abound, with wild trees of all sorts, and ebony; and the men are taller, handsomer, and longer lived than anywhere else."

Josephus, who will be quoted later in this chapter, states that Tacitus, the Roman historian, reveals a rumor that the Jews were descendants of the Ethiopians. Josephus's reference is correct, for writing circa 70 A.D., Tacitus does mention such a rumor, and declares that it was said by many: and it is worthy of note that Josephus did not at that point rush to refute the rumor or claim. If he felt that Tacitus was in error, he shows no sign of outrage because such a rumor was written; it is logical to assume, therefore, that Josephus saw no disgrace if somebody thought that he was a descendant of people whom later Europe called "Negroes."

In the introduction to the Bible that was prepared for the Philadelphia Bible House, it is stated that the actual writing of the Hebrew Scriptures is believed to have taken place in an epoch of about twelve hundred years. Some of the earliest poems of the Old Testament, it is thought, were composed as far back as 1200 A.D.; and James C. Muir[4] rightly says of the Bible, "These narratives reflect, rather than relate history." This is true, and we do not expect the Bible to reflect the history of mankind's beginnings; they do, however, bring to us Israel's explanation of how everything began.

The land of Cush (called Ethiopia in the text and Cush in the margin) found a place in the story of man's creation and the Garden of Eden. The second chapter of Genesis not only relates the facts concerning the making of the Garden of Eden, but also defines the location. The text says, "A river went out of Eden to water the Garden; and from thence it was parted, and became into four heads." The thirteenth verse of the same chapter says, "And the name of the second river is Gihon: The same it is that compasseth the whole land of Ethiopia."

Thus it is reflected in the Bible that Israel believed in the earliest existence of the black people's land, and we note that modern-day anthropology has arrived at the same conclusion. The findings of modern anthropology are summed up by Robert Ardrey:[5] "The home of our fathers was that African highland reaching north from the cape to the lakes of the Nile. Here we came about—slowly, ever so slowly—on a sky swept savannah glowing with menace."

The river referred to in the Genesis story might be either the Nile proper or the Albara, or some other Nile tributary. But over and above anthropological accuracy, the story points out the fact that ancient Israel held the blacks and their land in the same high regard as did the classical Greeks. It must be borne in mind that the ancient Hebrews were talking religion and not anthropology, and therefore their conclusions amount to a great deal more than merely the facing of tangible facts. They saw God at work in His creation proximately to what western writers knew as "Negroland," for Cush was black at the time that the creation story began to be circulated, and Israel knew it.

The second reference to "the land of blacks" appears in the biblical account of the patriarch Noah, his sons and grandsons. This is the story that was sinfully distorted by many racist preachers and laymen in colonial America, and is echoed in very recent sermons by Ku Klux Klan preachers. Colonial Christians taught that the people they called "Negroes" were descendants of Ham, and were under a curse because Ham was cursed.

Any examination of the story of Noah and sons reveals that God placed no curse upon anybody. The cursing that was done was done by Noah, and he placed no curse upon Ham, for, as Josephus says, Ham was near in blood. As the story goes, Noah, the Vineyard Keeper, became drunk on his wine, pulled off his clothes and lapsed into unconsciousness. His son Ham saw him in this condition and carried the news to his two brothers, Shem and Japheth. The latter two young men covered their nude father with a garment, while keeping their eyes turned away from his nudity. Later Noah "awoke from his wine," and learned (knew) that his son Ham had looked upon his nudity (and probably convulsed with laughter) which made him angry. In his anger Noah "put his mouth on"[6] Ham's youngest son, Canaan who might then have been snuggled in his father's arms, on his father's shoulders, or tugging at his father's knee. Noah said, "Cursed be Canaan; a servant of servants shall he be unto his brethren." Noah then added also that Canaan would be servant to Shem and Japheth.

We are told that Old Testament "experts" agree that Canaan was white,[7] and the descendants of Canaan were the same Canaanites that were inhabiting Palestine when Abraham came there to live; it was their land that Israel heard God promise to Abraham's seed. The various groups of Canaanites are called by their names in the Bible, but it is still explained that their overall name was Canaanites. There were Sidonions, sons of Heth, Jebusites, Amorites, Sinites, Arvadites, Zemanites, and Haamathites. In the Bible, God calls them by name as He promises their land to Abraham's seed, and it was they were slaughtered and suppressed during the conquests of Moses and Joshua. As late as I Chron. 4, the children of Simeon under Hezekiah's reign are still driving out the Canaanite inheritance of Ham. The whole Zionist movement, and the building of the Israeli nation of today, rests upon the promise that Israel heard God make to Abraham.

According to Israel, the wickedness of the Canaanite people caused God to doom them. Their iniquities are enumerated in various passages, and on the very day that Israel came out of Egypt, Moses mentions God's promise and names the nations who are to be driven out. He again declares in the Book of Deuteronomy that the Canaanite's own wickedness was to be their undoing. Israel was forbidden to make any covenant with these people or to exchange their sons and daughters in marriage with them. She was ordered to destroy all things pertaining to Canaanite religion, lest the Israelites be led astray by it. It always has been plain to all except bigots that the story of Noah's curse was Israel's way of accounting for that which was done to the owners of the land that Israel needed and wanted.

Ancient writers have found that Cushites (Ethiopians) descend from Ham's son Cush, who bore no curse from Noah, and who was actually one of the "brethren" to whom Canaan would be servant; thus when the Bible calls Ethiopians "the sons of Ham," it is referring to sons of Ham's son Cush, who was also the father of Nimrod "the Mighty Hunter": who was king of Mesopotamia. Cush also had other sons: Seba, Havilah, Sabtah, Raamah, Sheba and Sabtechah. The mapmakers have followed this interpretation of the Genesis story of the peopling of the earth, and their maps exhibit a tale of nations dispersed accordingly.[8]

It is to this goodly heritage that Josephus alludes when he says, "Time has not at all hurt the name of Chus; for the Ethiopians, over whom he reigned, are even at this day, both by themselves and by all men in Asia, called Chusites."[9]

There are various ways by which one people can show high regard for another, and one definite sign of high respect is by borrowing their customs; it is almost irrefutable that one of the Hebrew's most binding customs was borrowed from people that were black.

Abraham's father, Terah, moved his family out of Ur of the Chaldees with the stated intention of migrating to the land called Canaan, but he was overtaken by death during his sojourn in Haran. Afterwards God urged Abraham to leave Haran and go "unto a land that I will show thee"; so at the age of seventy-five, Abraham led his portion of the family into Canaan. Not long after Abraham settled in Canaan, a famine (probably a drought) forced him to go to Egypt and live for a while. It is affirmed by James C. Muir that this migration took place during the Hyksos period in Egypt, and he says that Abraham probably had an advantage, because it is believed that the Hyksos were of the same racial stock or of an allied stock to the Hittites. Possibly Abraham had been living among the Hittites, had spoken their language for years, and was now visiting a Hyksos-ruled country. Such circumstances could account for the reception that is recorded as having been given to Abraham's family by Pharaoh.

At any rate, Abraham returned from Egypt a wealthy man, and a vital part of that wealth consisted of a large group of servants and hired people, among whom was his wife's maid, Hagar. According to biblical account, Abraham's barren wife, Sarah, asked him to "go in unto" Hagar, the maid; and ten years following the return from Egypt, Hagar's son Ishmael was born to Abraham. At the age of ninety-nine years, when Isaac was only a promise from God not yet in his mother's womb, Abraham, obeying God's covenant command, underwent circumcision. He also administered it to thirteen-year-old Ishmael and to every male born in his household or purchased therefor; and he ordained that it should be perpetuated as an everlasting token of God's covenant with him. In this covenant God had promised to give Canaan to Abraham's progeny, and that many nations would come from his loins. It is important here to notice that Abraham underwent and instituted the ritual of circumcision after he had lived in Egypt, not before, even though God had earlier made to him the same promise in the same place— between Bethel and Hai.

Herodotus, the renowned scholar, in substantiating his belief that the Colchians were descended from Egyptians, based his conclusion mainly upon the fact that the Colchians practiced circumcision. He buttressed his argument by asserting the indisputable fact that the Egyptians and the Ethiopians (Cushites) were the only people who had practiced circumcision from the earliest times, adding that the Phoenicians and "the Syrians of Palestine"[10] confessed that they had learned the custom from the Egyptians. He further declared that he could not decide whether the Ethiopians had learned it from the Egyptians or whether Egyptians had learned it from the Ethiopians, because it had a very ancient origin in both countries. Let it be emphasized again that Herodotus went to these places and saw and studied the people and their customs approximately four hundred fifty years before Christ was born; and among tutored men everywhere, an eyewitness is a difficult witness to refute.

Josephus quotes from the above-mentioned passage in Herodotus's history, and after confirming that no other Syrians in Palestine practiced circumcision except the Jew, ends his comments with these words: "But as to such matters, let everyone speak what is agreeable to his own opinion." He does not attempt to refute it.

We now know that circumcision is indigenous to and universally practiced throughout the continent of Africa. this custom is one of the cornerstones of support to the proposition that in all areas of the continent are found the descendants of people who were driven northward and southward from the Sudanese-Saharan civilization when the Sahara began to dry up several thousand years ago. The origin of the custom lies so far in the remote history of Africa that there is no possibility of determining when it began. It is well established that in the settling of ancient Egypt, civilization came from the south, for the Sahara-Sudanese civilization flourished before the land of Egypt was born.

Before the slave trade came to its end, the missionaries, explorers, and tradesmen were traveling and living in sub-Saharan Africa. They were opening missions, charting rivers, measuring mountains, mapping the country and establishing trading posts. Following the Berlin Conference of 1884–5, the "scramble for Africa" brought European domination over the whole of the continent, with the exception of Liberia and modern Ethiopia. Eventually they penetrated every nation, state, tribe, and village, and even in the remotest places they found the ritual of circumcision and usually the ritual of clitoridectomy. Circumcision was found even in remote places that had no contact at all with Christianity, nor Islam, nor Judaism; and in all places the origins were too remote to determine when it began. The practice was not a religious ritual as we understand religious rituals; however, to the African, religion was all of life. Circumcision was a necessary process in the making of a proper man.

It is not at all ridiculous to see the likelihood that Hagar, the Egyptian, confronted Abraham over and over with the fact that their son Ishmael was lacking in something vital to the body of a properly constituted man, and that he, Abraham, was also. (After all, she had personal knowledge). There is no logic that can reasonably argue that Abraham had lived in Egypt, made friends, and acquired servant families without knowing that circumcision was unfailingly practiced among Egyptians and Cushites. This helps to explain why a ninety-nine-year-old man saw no risk in obeying such a command from God. It is inconceivable that a ninety-nine-year-old man would perform such an operation upon himself, his son, and all the men of his household the very same day if he did not know that they would survive. The size of Abraham's household can be somewhat determined by the fact that he armed three hundred eighteen "trained servants" when he went to rescue Lot from the coalition of the five kings that sacked Sodom and Gomorrah. A careful reading of the text will reveal that God did not use the language of risk in ordering Abraham to circumcise. The great act of faith lay in undergoing a covenant ritual that would vitally involve a son to be born to him long after this man and wife had passed the age of such possibilities. Even if Abraham had had enough faith to perform a heretofore unknown operation upon himself, it seems certain that some of the other three hundred eighteen men would have balked or fled, and their wives with them.

The evidence strongly indicates that Abraham knowingly adopted an African ritual-custom, and he made it the only tangible feature that would distinguish the Hebrew from other men, for they came in all colors, sizes and human forms. It holds until this day, for to this day all that is necessary to become a Jew is to profess an adhering faith in the Lord God of Abraham, Isaac and Jacob, and to undergo the ritual of circumcision. In today's world, and for various reasons, men of all faiths and in all areas practice circumcision. Nothing said to the contrary can obliterate the fact that because of Abraham's faith in God, he became the channel through which the black man gave circumcision to the world.

There is one intimation that some Old Testament people believed that the black people were under the special care of God. For example, the prophet Amos did say to Israel, "Are ye not as Children of the Ethiopians Unto Me, O children of Israel? Saith the Lord. Have not I brought up Israel out of the land of Egypt? and the Philistines from Caphtor, and the Syrians from Kir?"[11]

Finally we repeat the words of Josephus: "Time has not at all hurt the name of Chus."

Questions

1. According to the Old Testament, why did the Canaanites lose their land?
2. Name the two most widely quoted Old Testament passages concerning black people (Ethiopians).
3. According to Lerone Bennett, Jr., how were blacks regarded by the ancient world?
4. In Greek mythology, to what land did the gods repair for an annual twelve-day feast?
5. Did Old Testament writers know that Cush was of ancient origin?
6. Who were supposed to be the accursed children of Ham?
7. Who said, "Time has not hurt the name of Chus"? (Cush or Kush)?
8. Of what nationality was Hagar, Abraham's concubine?
9. How do we know where the custom of circumcision began?
10. How many males did Abraham circumcise in one day?

Notes

1. Psalm 87.

2. *Before the Mayflower.*

3. *Ibid.*

4. From the archeological notes on the Bible, in the Bible published by The Philadelphia Bible House.

5. Robert Ardrey, *African Genesis* (New York: Dell, 1961), p. 9.

6. An old Southern expression used by Afro-Americans. The expressions grew out of their belief that only God could curse or put a curse upon.

7. Herbert Aptheker, *Afro-American History: The Modern Era* (New York: The Citadel Press, 1971), p. 30.

8. Rand McNally's *Historical Atlas of The Holy Lands* is one of many sources.

9. Josephus, *The Antiquities of the Jews*, Book 1, Chapter VI.

10. Rawlinson, George, Trans., *The History of Herodotus*, Second Book, Euterpe (Chicago: University of Chicago Press, 1952), p. 104.

11. Amos 9:7.

6

THE MIXED MULTITUDE

I N DESCRIBING THE GREAT host of people who followed Moses out of the land of Egypt, the Book of Exodus (12:38) brings to us a very revealing matter in this statement: "And A Mixed Multitude went up also with them." This chapter will be devoted to a study of the Hebrews and the "Mixed Multitude" that made up the nation of people afterwards called "the children of Israel." The results of such a study are often surprising and maybe controversial at some points, yet a fair examination of the situation must take all facts into consideration.

The Book of Genesis (47:9) paints a beautiful picture of an old man, Jacob, around one hundred and thirty years of age hearing the news that a son, long regarded as lost, was yet alive, living in Egypt and getting along extremely well. He learned that his once-favored son Joseph, last seen when only seventeen years of age, was governor of Egypt, and that he was insisting that the entire family pull up stakes and move to Egypt in order to share the fortune that he had found in that strange land. The old man was so shaken by the sudden turn of events that he led the entire family to a very special place to worship and seek assurances from God. He went to the city of Beersheba, "and offered sacrifices unto the God of his father Isaac."

Beersheba was the southernmost area of Canaan, and the scene of sojourn of other members of the patriarchal family. Hagar and Ishmael had thirstily wandered in the "wilderness of Beersheba," Gen. 21;14) and it was here that God opened the eyes of faithful Hagar so that she found water to slake the dying thirst of her son, who had been rejected by his own father. At Beersheba, God heard Ishmael's voice, and the Angel of God calmed Hagar's fears and promised to make her son a great nation. Abraham dug a well and named it "the well of the oath" (Beersheba) and planted a tree to commemorate the promise of good will among himself, Abimelech, king of the Philistines, and Phicol, chief captain of the latter's army. It was a special place of worship for Abraham (Gen. 21:33).

Isaac, the father of Jacob, was driven by famine to the Philistine city of Gerar, and there he pretended that his wife was his sister. He became prosperous and was asked to leave, and after digging wells called Esek, Sitnah, and Rehoboth, he finally dug one at Beersheba that was not taken away from him. He found water, called it "an oath" (Shebak), and built there an altar of God.

Having received assurances from God that his seed would become a nation in Egypt, that they would return, and that he would die in peace, Jacob was placed in wagons sent for the purpose by Pharaoh of Egypt, and he began the fateful journey into Egypt. There were sixty-six people in Jacob's extended family in Canaan (Gen. 46:26–7), and they joined Joseph, his wife, and his two sons, bringing the Hebrews' total to seventy people.

According to the King James Version of the Bible, that day that Jacob blessed Pharaoh (Gen. 47:7) began a Hebrew sojourn in Egypt that lasted four hundred thirty years; however, there is some controversy concerning the accuracy of the Hebrew length of stay as given in the King James Bible. Josephus put the length of the Israelite sojourn in Egypt at two hundred fifteen years, and argues that the four hundred thirty year figure covers the entire period between Abraham's migration into Canaan and the Hebrew exodus from Egypt. The Josephus point of view is upheld by one of his translators.[1] The translator's footnote indicates that both the Samaritan text of the Hebrew Scripture and the Septuagint translation state the same length of time as does Josephus. The translator first argues that this date comes from scholars working with the Masora, the same source used by the King James scholars.

The Masora or Masorah is defined and described as the Hebrew tradition, formed gradually through a succession of centuries, setting forth the correct form of the text of The Scriptures, or the collection of critical notes in which the correct text is embodied. The term Masora (or Masorah) derives from two other Hebrew terms meaning "to fetter" and to "hand down."[2] It dates perhaps from the time of Ezra to about 930 A.D. Its purpose was to safeguard the integrity of the biblical text. It was this body of scholarship that divided the Bible into chapters and verses; fixed the spelling, pronunciation and cantillation of words and texts. The text itself was left unchanged because it is forbidden in Deut. 13:1 to add to the Holy Scriptures, but the Masora prescribed the manner of organizing the content.

Whether one uses the four hundred thirty year figure or the two hundred fifteen year figure to denote the number of years that Israel stayed in Egypt the present study will not be affected, because this study is based upon the King James translation which always uses the four hundred thirty year figure.

All sources agree with the fact that Jacob's family consisted of seventy people when they moved into Egypt. This family total is given in Genesis, Exodus and in later writings. They had entered Egypt as a group of seventy, but by the time of the Exodus the family had grown into a nation of approximately two and a half million people. The Bible gives us no figure at all to cover the entire population, but it does give us the firm foundation upon which to base our calculation of the full number of the Israelites.

It is first stated in Exodus 12:37 that Israel left Egypt with "about six hundred thousand on foot that were men, beside children," and Exodus 38:26 drops the term "about" saying that the census found 603,550 men "from twenty years old and upward." The opening verse of the Book of Numbers states that during the second month of the second year of their pilgrimage, God ordered Moses to take a census of "every male by their polls; from twenty years old and upward, all that are able to go forth to war in Israel," and again the total came to 603,550 men.

It is plainly shown that the figures listed above accounted only for Israel's army duty potentialities. It does not include females at all, and the custom of not bothering to count females is carried throughout the account of Israel's history. There were males also that were not counted, and they fall in several categories. We have no way of knowing how many men there were who were of the age for war, but were exempted under Mosaic law. That there were exemptions we know from reading Deuteronomy 20:5–9 and 24:5, wherein exemptions are extended to men with houses too recently built to have been dedicated; to men who had not eaten of their vineyards; to men with new wives and unconsummated marriages; and to men whose fears and faintheartedness might be contagious. Some of these conditions for exemptions could not have prevailed in their nomadic stage in the wilderness, but at least two of them might have.

Other males who were not counted included those who were unable to go to war by reason of physical illness, and we must mention the males under twenty years old. We must never forget that the totals given us do not include the priestly tribe of Levi.[3] These belonged to God, and to Him they were the ransom instead of all the firstborn. (Num. 3:12–13) They were given to Aaron and to the tabernacle service, which was vital to the Children of Israel (Num. 3:9). They were later counted, but the count was not included in the overall figures rendered by census. In estimating the total number of people who left Egypt, we must follow the principle given to us by many sociologists and others of allowing at least four people for every male. In other words, we must base our estimation upon the allowance of four members per family as average. This would estimate that for the average family there would be husband, wife and two children. Family sizes varied, of course, but the estimated average of four is a sound one. In order then to arrive at an overall figure, we must multiply the number of potential soldiers by four and add the total men and women of the Levitical tribe, and lo, we behold a mighty host of over two-and-a-half million souls.

There can be no grounds for doubting that the writers of the Torah intended to use the figures that they have given to us, because practically the same figures are mentioned several times as noted above. There is at least one other time that the figures are mentioned, and by Moses himself. His followers had complained because of their desire for meat, and God had promised Moses that their complaint would be answered by a generous supply. Such a prospect was incomprehensible to the mind of Moses, and he makes it known to God in Numbers 11:21; "And Moses said, the people, among whom I am, are six hundred thousand footmen; and Thou hast said, I will give them flesh, that they may eat for a whole month. Shall the flocks and the herds be slain for them, to suffice them?"

It is more than merely obvious that Exodus multitude could not have grown to such huge proportions by the Hebrew birthrate. Jacob's family started in Egypt with seventy members, and in the short space of four hundred thirty years could not possibly have engendered six hundred thousand footmen and their families, in spite of the fact that in earlier days such an explanation has been rendered by teachers. These ideas were based upon the supposed fecundity of the ancient Hebrew. They argued that the Israelites were more prolific than most other people, and that the population grew rapidly as a consequence.

These teachers, of course, have been those who believed or wanted to believe that all who followed Moses out of Egypt were Hebrews, an impossible fact to support.

An examination of the families of biblical personalities reveals that before and after the Exodus, Hebraic procreativity was no greater than ordinary for any agrarian people, and it can be said that there are indications leading us to believe that some sub-Saharan African people were even more productive than the Israelites. Abraham had eight sons born to him by two wives and one concubine. Isaac had two sons that were borne by one wife. Jacob had twelve sons and one daughter, born to him by two wives and two concubines, and so on. The history of the Hebrews shows that family sizes varied in ordinary fashion, some having large families and some couples having no children at all. For example, I Chronicles 4:27 tells us that one Shimei had sixteen sons and six daughters, "but his brethren had not many children, neither did all their family multiply, like the children of Judah." During the period of the Judges, Gideon had seventy sons and Jair had thirty sons, but these were very exceptional and rare instances; and even if this had been the average, the Israelites could still not have increased from seventy to two-and-a-half million in less than five hundred years, especially if there were any death rate at all.

Under the marriage laws of the Israelites, girls generally married early, but men generally married in full maturity, as was the case with Esau (Gen. 26:34), who married at the age of forty years. Why this custom prevailed is not quite clear, but it would seem that a man could only achieve individual security around this age in life, because the father was the head of the house and sole owner of the family enterprise. The girl's lot was one of complete dependency, and in a polygynous society her role would not require full maturity at the beginning of marriage. However, neither polygyny nor concubinage could account for the miraculous increase of the Israelites in Egypt.

That there was a tremendous non-Hebrew presence in the

Exodus host becomes even more apparent when we take the time
to examine and to compare the tribal summaries. As was pointed
out earlier, the first "numbering" of the tribes took place in the
Sinai desert during their second year of travel. The second
"numbering" took place in the plains of Moab around thirty-nine
years later; and by this time the numbers had been reduced by
various scourges and catastrophes, the worst being the epidemic
or "plague" that swept away twenty-four thousand souls in
Shittim (Numb. 25:9). The chart that follows shows the changes
in growth rate during the interval.

Population Chart

Tribe	Number of Sons	Sinai Totals	Moab Totals (Num. 26)	Changes
Reuben	4	46,500	43,730	-2,700
Simeon	5	59,300	22,200	-37,100
Gad	7	45,650	40,500	-5,150
Judah	3	74,600	76,500	+1,900
Issachar	4	54,400	64,300	+9,800
Zebulon	3	57,400	60,500	+3,100
Ephraim	3	40,500	32,500	-8,000
Manasseh	1	32,500	52,700	+20,200
Benjamin	5	35,400	45,600	+10,200
Dan	1	62,700	64,500	+1,800
Ashur	3	41,500	53,400	+11,900
Napthali	4	53,400	45,400	-8,000
Total warriors	43	603,550	601,730	-1,820
Levitical tribe	3	24,300	23,000	-1,300
Grand totals	46	627,850	624,730	-3,120

The population chart of the tribal summaries of the Israelites
shows that a man started out with seven sons, and less than five
hundred years later there are more than 45,000 people. Another
man started out with three sons, and in the same length of time
there are 57,000 people; while still another started out with three
sons and now there are over 74,000 people; and finally Dan

started out with one son and ends up with over 62,000 people. This chart alone prohibits any reasonable mind from concluding that the census involves only people with Hebrew genes, and anyone who can believe that one man could produce a progeny of 62,000 people in less than five hundred hears has learned things about human life that are unknown to everybody else in the universe.

The answer to the question as to where did so many people come from finds its most decisive clue in the Exodus account of Israel's departure from Egypt. The title for this chapter, as has been said, is taken from Exodus 12:38 which says, "And a mixed multitude went up also with them"' and the marginal note renders this as "a great mixture" went up with them. The confusion lies largely in the phrase "went up with them," for there is no account anywhere in the Bible of an Exodus group that was separate and apart from the group called "the Children of Israel,"[4] except Hobab's family. All "numbering" or census-taking places every living soul in a family and a tribal group. The same is true in the mustering of troops, the deployment of troops, elections, and congregational assemblies. This means that any "mixed multitude" of people were members of an Israelite family and a member of some tribe. The situation as it is invariably projected in the Scripture would find clearer understanding if the translation were rendered simply "And there went up a mixed multitude," or "there went up a great mixture of people"; truly the people known as "the Children of Israel" were themselves a "mixed multitude." In fact it was the "mixed" and not the Hebrew that made up the multitude. It is likely that the multitude was "mixed" in race, color, and national origin. It appears that all non-white colors were indigenous to the children of Israel.

The presence of the "mixed multitude" could in some measure account for the fact that Moses found it so difficult to bring about conformity in religion, and in the observance of rules that were peculiar to Hebrew culture. He propounded legislation dealing with just about every facet of their lives, and he regulated virtually every possible relationship among people. Moses taught his followers with a meticulosity befitting only to a situation wherein most of the people were hearing it for the first time, and in spite of all his efforts, there was still great difficulty in achieving conformity. It was for Moses almost an impossible task.

The demand for material idols that forced Aaron, in the absence of Moses, to make the golden calf can be viewed as a clear example of the influence that was exerted by the "mixed multitude." Hand made idols were never a part of Hebrew religion. Abraham believed in God as revealed in the soul, and he built an altar, not an idol. Isaac and Jacob conceived of God in the same way and manner as did Abraham before them. A West Coast minister[5] would point out that Abraham's sons by Keturah conceived of God as Abraham did, and that there in the land of Midian Moses learned the nature of God and the true name by which He would be called (Exod. 6:2–3). Jethroe the Medianite worshipped God as unseen to human eyes, and built an altar for worship (Exod. 18:12). In all the wanderings of the patriarchs and throughout their Egyptian sojourn, there is no mention of man-made idols among the Hebrews. During the Exodus experience, it continued as God's ruling "Ye Shall Not Make with me Gods of silver, Neither Shall Ye make unto you gods of Gold." (Exod. 20:23) At a very late pre-Christian date, Tacitus[6] the Roman said, "The Jews have no notion of anymore than one Divine Being; and that known only in the mind."

The golden calf incident yields two pertinent ideas. In the first place, that must have been a large and formidable group that gathered around Aaron saying, "Up make us Gods, which shall go before us; for as for this fellow Moses, the man that brought us up out of the land of Egypt, we wot not what is become of him." (Exod. 32:1) Evidently the demanding group was too large to be dealt with by Aaron in any other manner save appeasement, and it is unthinkable that the Hebraic element would make such a demand. This fact of the incident could be taken as an indication that the non-Hebrew element had the majority power. Secondly, when the multitude demanded a hand made idol, Aaron knew exactly what to make. He knew to construct the golden calf, because he had no doubt seen many of the local gods of Egypt represented in animal form, as was the case in ancient Egypt.[7] Aaron was keen enough to include a portion of the Hebrew taste in worship by building an altar, something to which they were accustomed. Another reference from Tacitus says: "The Egyptians worship abundance of animals, and images of various sorts."

The other element to be considered was the nudity of the people dancing around the golden calf, and to note that it was suggested by Aaron. (Exod. 32:25) Here again we see something foreign to the worship and culture of the patriarchs, and it must have come from a tropical zone. Nudity might possibly have been noted in certain instances in the tropical countries, but we must recall that the Hebrew Bible claims that all the nations of Canaan had been condemned because a man looked upon the nudity of his father.

At a later date, Joshua seems to be mindful of the former religion of the "mixed multitude" when he admonished Israel saying, "And put away the Gods which your fathers served on the other side of the flood, and in Egypt." (Josh. 24:10) The Prophet Ezekiel indicates the general knowledge of the same former custom when he mentions "The idols of Egypt," (Ezek. 20:7–8) and sounds as if he meant that they were never totally abandoned. Most of his twenty-third chapter reads as if the northern Israelites were the more prone to retain strains of Egyptian worship.

Another difficulty in achieving conformity among the "mixed multitude" surfaces again at a place called "Taberah" (Num. 11). Here it is actually stated that the "mixed multitude" started the trouble (Num. 11:4). It was they who began to vocalize their desire for meat in their diet, and the others were influenced by them. This vocalized desire led to the death of some fourteen thousand people, who feasted upon the flesh of quails that had drifted away from the sea and perished.

There is yet another story on the point of the mixed multitude that had a tragic ending for one man. There was an incident as related in Leviticus 24:10–16, wherein two men got into a personal fight, and one of them "blasphemed the name of the Lord and cursed." Moses ordered the young man held in custody (put in the ward), while taking some time to give thought as to what the penalty should be. Moses made a drastic decision, and upon his order the lad was speedily executed by the congregation. This story is very pertinent to the chapter because the condemned lad was the son of "an Israelitish woman, whose father was an Egyptian." Here is positive proof that Egyptians were in the Exodus movement.

The final instance to be cited as having the remote possibility of being related to the presence of the "mixed multitude" occurred about three hundred years following the Exodus. The twelfth chapter of Judges tells of a quarrel and a battle between the Ephraimites and the Gileadites, the latter being under the command of Jephthah. The Gileadites were the victors, and being in command of the Jordan fording places, they arrested, examined and killed all people found to have been Ephraimites. Identity was established through a test which consisted of the correct pronunciation of the word "Shibboleth," the Hebrew term for "stream" or "flood." The test was workable because the Ephraimites could not shape their mouths for form the "sh," and their use of the word came out "sibboleth." It is indeed strange to find such a difference in the ability to pronounce a term among people who were members of the same nation, and who lived together so closely. Perhaps the first key leading to an understanding of this variation is carried in the slur that was hurled at the Gileadites by the Ephraimites. It is recorded in Verse 4 that "The men of Gilead smote Ephraim because they said 'Ye Gileadites are fugitives of Ephraim among the Ephraim-

ites and among the Manassites.'" Both the enmity and the slur
might conceivably date back to the discovery that somewhere
between the first and second numberings of the tribes of Israel,
the tribe of Mannasseh, from whom the Gileadites descend,
gained twenty thousand men; while during the same period eight
thousand were lost by the tribe of Ephraim, and ten thousand
were lost by the tribe of Benjamin.

It is an inescapable conclusion that the most generous
reasonable estimates or calculation can find less than fourteen
thousand people in the Exodus population who had any Hebrew
blood (genes) at all! The evidence at hand demonstrates beyond
all reasonable doubt that they who were called "the Children of
Israel" were a heterogeneous people, with no single bloodline,
and predominately of non-Hebrew or non-Asian descent. They
were a mixed nation of people drawn together by domestic
relationships and a common bond of suffering, and led by a
Hebrew minority segment who had wealth and an imperishable
desire to seek what was know to them as "The Promised Land."
It was their adopted homeland, and they had nourished a desire
to go there and build an independent nation in which there
would be "one law" among them. Their venture will forever
stand out as history's uniquely splendid example of the building
of a truly democratic nation. Here we see the "melting pot"
working out as a "melting pot" should, and until this very day
it remains impossible to determine which individual Israelites
actually carry Jacob's genes and which do not. So the Jew will
live on, and will prosper and grow under any and all conditions
because of Judaism's ability to be a unified people. There will
continue to be, as in the past, causes and issues that will bring
divisions among these people, of course; but such divisions will
never be based upon genetic distribution. Among the children of
Israel there can be no minority groups in the American sense of
the word, therefore they cannot be destroyed by the elsewhere
eternal warfare engendered by race, color, or national origin.

The questions concerning the origins and closer identification of the Children of Israel were dealt with by some of the Gentile writers of ancient times. Josephus himself quotes from Manetho, said by him and other sources to have been an Egyptian scholar who had mastered Greek language and learning. Manetho wrote about the different groups of Hyksos or shepherd kings who once ruled Egypt. According to Josephus, Manetho said that the Hyksos rulers were driven out after a long reign. There was a portion of them, however, who did not flee from Egypt immediately, but took refuge in a redoubt that contained ten thousand acres of territory. Thummosis (Thutmoses), king of Egypt, failed in his attempt to invade the doubt, and therefore agreed to allow them to leave Egypt voluntarily and unharmed. Two hundred fifty thousand left. Josephus also says that Manetho's second book refers to these Hyksos as "captives," and because of this designation Josephus asserts that they were the Hebrews.

However, the weight of history and scholarship makes it quite unlikely that the Hebrews and the Hyksos were one and the same. They were undoubtedly closely allied because of Joseph, but the Hyksos and Hebrews were two different groups of people, and the dethroned shepherd kings would either have run or died. Certainly among the children of Israel there must have been some Asians present, but there are no grounds for determining any number as large as two hundred fifty thousand, this coupled with the fact that the Hyksos were driven out of Egypt while the Pharaoh sought to keep the Israelites in Egypt.

In another place, Josephus appropriates a quotation from the writings of one Cherilus, who saw a body of troops marching with the Persians against the Greeks. According to Josephus, the following quotation makes it evident to him that Cherilus is writing about Jews: "At the last there passed over a people, wonderful to be beheld; for they spoke the Phoenician tongue with their mouths; they dwelt in the Solymean Mountains, near a broad lake. Their heads were sooty; they had round rasures on them; Their heads and faces were like nasty horse heads also, that had been hardened in the smoke." And for any study dealing with the colors among Israelites, it is important to note that Josephus, the Jew, sees a reference to his people in descriptions like "sooty heads," and with heads and faces looking like they had been hardened in the smoke. To Josephus, Jews might possibly looked like this—"smoky."

Tacitus, [8] who has been referred to as a Roman historian, wrote about the origin, the history and the religion of the Jews, and like a good scholar, quotes from the opinions of other writers whose works were available in his day. One part of his statement says this: "Some say they were a people that were very numerous in Egypt, under the reign of Isis; and that the Egyptians got free of that burden, by sending them into the adjacent countries, under their captains, Hierosolymus and Judas." Some parts of this quotation are true to the Bible account. It was true that the devastating plagues made Israel a burden unto Pharaoh and Egypt, in spite of the fact that the Israelites wanted to leave and Pharaoh prevented them. It is also true that following the death of the Egyptian firstborn, Pharaoh this time called for Moses and Aaron and said, "Rise up, and get you forth from among my people, both ye and the Children of Israel; and go, serve the Lord, as ye have said . . . And the Egyptians were urgent upon the people, that they might send them out of the land in haste; for they said, we be all dead men." (Exod. 12:30–33) It would be expected that pharaonic records would say that the Israelites were sent away for the benefit of Egypt, and Egyptian historians might be expected to have quoted it in that manner.

The latter part of the above quotation from Tacitus, written in 70 A.D., says boldly: "*The Greatest Part* (most writers) say they were those Ethiopians whom fear and hatred obliged to change their habitation, in the reign of Cephas."

This reminds us that Egypt had annexed the land of Cush to them circa 2200 B.C., had seen them regain freedom when the Hyksos invaded Egypt, but had reannexed the Cushites after the Hyksos were driven out. This was done through military action and must have involved some suppression and fearfulness, for the Cushites (Ethiopians) were a conquered people. What are we to conclude when people as late as 70 A.D. looked at Jews and believed them to have been descendants of Ethiopians? The Greek term "Ethiopian" means "black" or literally "burnt-faced," and the only way to decide that a person or a people were Ethiopians would be by sight identification. The fact that the opinion was not ridiculous to Tacitus must have been because it supported what he saw when he saw Israelites. From the beginning of recorded history until today, the presence of the black gene is more unmistakable where found than is any other gene in the world. No one ever called another "black" through mistake. America today opposes and fears intermarriage between whites and blacks because the black gene is irrepressible; it evidences itself unto an unknown number of generations. In South Africa there is no hesitancy at all in this matter; if one *looks* black he *is* black. What else can be said?

The Abington Commentary concludes its discussion of Exodus 12:38 by saying: "The mixed company must have included Egyptians and other co-laborers, who may have intermarried with them and now sought with them this way to freedom."

When all the available facts are examined, we know beyond doubt that the black presence was one of the dominant elements in the original native Egyptian population, and furthermore we know that the Cushite (Ethiopian) formed a large part in the Egyptian population of Israel's day. In truth, it must be admitted that Moses perhaps led more black people out of Egypt than those of other colors. We understand with little wonder why the Judaic lawgiver decreed, "Thou Shalt not abhor an Egyptian; because thou was a stranger in his land."[9]

The black presence in Israel was perhaps somewhat diluted with the passing of many centuries, but it could not have disappeared. The black or partially black children of Israel must have been scattered over the Old Testament world in the depopulation of Samaria and in the Babylonian diaspora.

Centuries later, those in whom there remained a high black visibility could not have fled into Europe and blended into Europe's color pattern, so they must have remained in those pockets of Judaism that were allowed to exist after the Muslim conquest of the Middle East. It is certain that the bulk of the black Israelites either lived by accepting the religion of Islam or died under the Islamic invasion before they had the chance to convert.

Today we see only the white descendants of the Children of Israel because many of them had settled in Europe before the Muslims invaded the Middle East and many others fled deeper into Europe as the Muslims conquered Spain and marched half way across France.

There can be no objection to the idea that European intermarriage contributed a great deal to the appearance of the Jews during the early Christian era and during the Middle Ages. The apostle Paul was himself a product of marriage between an Israelite and a European, and it is certain that this kind of mating expanded greatly after the Hebrew was forced to seek homeland in Europe. Many of the white and black Israelites died in the Spanish Inquisition; while many of the white ones fled, the black ones could not flee into Europe in large groups, and they were no doubt forcibly converted to Islam. Some of the results of these black genes can likely be seen to this day in groups like the Bedoins that were once quite visible in Jerusalem and other Palestinian cities and in other areas of the Middle East.

Questions
1. How many were in Jacob's family when he went to live in Egypt?
2. According to the Old Testament how long were the Israelites in Egypt?
3. How many able-bodied men left Egypt with Moses?
4. What males were not counted in the "numberings" of Israel?
5. Did Hebrew religion permit idol worship?

6. Did Egyptian religion permit idol worship?
7. Give the ethnic background of the first man that Moses ordered executed for blasphemy.
8. What was the Hebrew "Promised Land"? Promised by whom to whom?
9. What finally happened to the Hyksos who ruled Egypt?
10. What caused the Israelites to be scattered over the known world?
11. What has possibly become of the black Israelites that were scattered over the then-known world?

Notes

1. Flavius Josephus, *The Antiquities of the Jews*, Book 2, trans. William Whiston (Grand Rapids, Mich.: Kregel Publications, 1960).
2. R.J. Zwi Werblowsky and Geoffrey Wigdor, *The Encyclopedia of the Jewish Religion* (New York: Holt, Rinehart and Winston, 1966), p. 253.
3. Numbers 1:47.
4. The next chapter deals with the Kenites, the descendants of Hobab.
5. The Rev. J. Mayo Roberts.
6. *History of the Jews*, Book 5, Chapter 2, Flavius Josephus.
7. Geoffrey Parrinder, *Religion in Africa* (Baltimore: Penguin Books, 1969).
8. *Ibid.*
9. Deuteronomy 23:7.

7

THE CHILDREN OF ISRAEL

THE PRECEDING CHAPTER analyzed the statistics of the Exodus population and the possible indications involved in the phrase, "the mixed multitude." It was concluded that many people in the Exodus population must have been black native-stock Egyptians, and it was also thought that the Cushite was not uncommon among them.

The present chapter must of necessity deal with some of the factors that made possible the tremendous growth of the Israelites during their Egyptian sojourn. The Bible account makes no attempt to explain the phenomenal population expansion, but it does give us some knowledge of events, customs, and situations that could have and most certainly did pave the way for an extended family to become a nation. It must be kept in mind that the Egyptian masses were oppressed and impoverished during Israel's good years and would naturally have been the reservoir from which the Israelite population drew very largely.

The most sustaining and most potent survival growth factor

for the Children of Israel was their belief that one day they would return and conquer Canaan, "The Promised Land." On at least two occasions God had promised Abraham that his seed would someday possess and rule Canaan, and the same promise was communicated and renewed to Isaac and Jacob. In fulfillment of a promise exacted from them, the children of Israel carried the body of Jacob back to the family cemetery in Canaan, and Joseph later forced from them a promise to carry his bones to Canaan with them on their final return to that land. Moses fulfilled the promise.

The dream of a promised land was not only the adhesive agent that cemented Israel's community into oneness, it also served to make them an aggressively progressive and prosperous people. It prohibited them from becoming complacent even during their very good days in Egypt, and it also stifled the rise of any sentiment or temptation to lose their separate identity. This dream converted Moses, for he believed in the promise and its land. In his very conversion itself, God commissioned him to lead the people out of Egypt to Canaan and named the people who were to be displaced (Exod. 3:8, 17) before Israel could occupy the land.

The dream of forever possessing Canaan gave rise to the messianic hope of many, many centuries later when the days were dark for a scattered, subjugated Hebrew, and it operates in the Jewish mind and community even in this day. When it is said that we should give America back to the Indians from whom it was taken less than five hundred years ago, it is taken as evidence of the insincerity of the speaker; but the Jew felt that it was by divine right that he returned to displace the people now called Arabs, many of whom had lived in the land since the depopulation of Samaria by Shalmaneser the Assyrian, nearly eight hundred years before Christ came. Every individual Jew is committed to the welfare and survival of the new Israel, and no amount of good or bad fortune can cause one segment of Jewry to work or cause the destruction of the other. God's promise includes each and every Jew, and it serves to hold the nation together. The rise in class and caste among them is impossible. The most wealthy and powerful Jew in the world would never think of being addressed by other Jews as "Lord," nor would he look upon his co-religionists as "commoners."

This dream of someday possessing a faraway land must have had a profound effect upon the people among whom the Israelites lived in Egypt. To every slave, every servant, every family-less person, every downtrodden soul in proximity, Israel could say, "We have a land promised to us by the God of our fathers; come with us and we will do thee good." And as this influenced Hobab in Midian, it is reasonable to believe that it impressed others in Egypt.

The cherished name "the Children of Israel" was born in Egypt, and the chronicler used it to designate the group that had become mighty in number. It does not seem to designate the one family. When he was alone in Egypt, Joseph was referred to as a Hebrew (Gen. 39:14, 40:15, 41:12, 43:32), and there were later occasions when the term "Hebrew" was used in Egypt; but the term "Hebrew" gradually gave way to the boarder designation of "the Children of Israel," and after the death of Joseph this term is used consistently.

In order to find some understanding as to how one Hebrew family grew to nationhood proportions in such a short span of years, it is necessary to analyze the makeup of that family and to delve as deeply as possible into its known history. We must also sift through the events and customs found among the Hebrew people and the Egyptians, also. It is a difficult task to determine with any assurance those factors that must have aided Israel's growth, and in doing so it must always be borne in mind that Egypt was their only reservoir of human resources. No people were drawn from Asia, for at the time of the Exodus, the multitude was already amassed and moving as a national unit.

Over and over it is to be pointed out that the Hyksos kings from Asia were ruling Egypt when Abraham visited there, when

Joseph was sold there as a slave, and when Jacob moved the family to that land. The conquering Hyksos left no record of indications of having transplanted any population. They did not come as colonists, but as conquerors and rulers. They lived as despots over a nation of people who had never before been conquered thusly and who had undergone very little ethnic change since their earliest existence as a people. Although the Hyksos rulers are referred to as Egyptians in the Bible, the reader must bear in mind that they were aliens and outsiders who tyrannized an indigenous population. Their sway outlasted the lifetime of the patriarch Joseph. They held their kingship for at least, or nearly, a century after Joseph died. They held sway until "There arose a new King that knew not Joseph."

The way and manner in which young Joseph went into Egypt and the conditions under which he lived during his earliest days there give us a true picture of what slavery was like in Egypt, and in fact, throughout the continent of Africa.

So many American writers and chattel slavery apologists have sought to find the roots of such slavery in Africa and have managed to plant this thought in the minds of myriads of well-meaning people. Since learning that from time immemorial human beings were bought and sold in Africa, the apologists have tried to paint a picture of a savage, brutal place wherein there was such a harsh system of slavery, that kidnapped Africans were already suited to the brutalities of American slavery before they reached its unhappy shores. They blame the African for the fact that American slavery could exist, declaring that the captive was readily adaptable to American slavery because all or most of them had suffered the same fate in their homeland. These are the same writers, incidentally, who tend to cling to and support the myth that the black American was docile and already tempered to slavery's yoke. This entire argument is false, of course, and has been completely refuted by all writers of African history, and by all honest men who write American history.

The concept of chattel slavery did not originate in Africa, and it rarely existed, if at all, anywhere on the continent prior to the high-point years of the Atlantic slave trade; even at that late date the few instances that were in any way approaching chattel slavery were found in those African states whose very existence was based upon the trade itself. A kind of slavery that was different from traditional was found in the regions of Dahomey and Calabar, whose prominence was owed to their wholehearted participation in the Atlantic slave trade itself and whose history prior to their slave trade activity is almost completely obscured.

The savage concept of turning human beings into chattel property came from a later than African civilization which flourished on another continent. It seems that this insane concept grew out of the demented minds of the Romans during the days of the empire. Some apologists would like very much to explain the rise and growth of chattel in socioeconomic terms, but those who were victims of the system and those who have been the victims of its vestiges know differently. These people know that a very serious psychological deficiency was and is at work in both chattel slavery and in the vestiges of chattel slavery. Any man in any age under any culture or set of conditions who could conceive of another human being in the form of chattel property suffered from a streak of insanity. Any man under any set of circumstances who has the slightest desire to hold onto any vestiges of the chattel aftermath is suffering from the same streak of insanity. Thomas Jefferson put it all too mildly in saying that chattel slavery has developed "odious peculiarities" in the slave holders and all those who were and are likeminded. Nobody on earth can claim to have a well and healthy mind when it is ravished with bigotry, and any person who desires to mistreat a man because that person's grandfather mistreated the man's grandfather is in need of psychiatry from another culture.

The African form of servitude cannot truthfully be called slavery, for while it is true that human beings were taken, bought and sold, it is also true that they were bought and sold to members of households. Basil Davidson says that they were in truth "vassals," and these servants were members of family groups, although their positions in the household were subordinate. This has been more accurately called domestic slavery or servitude, because the person in the subordinate position was under the protection and responsibility of the family and its head. Such persons could and usually did marry in the family, and where there were no sons, a male servant became the head of the family upon the death of the father. This custom was found also among the Hebrews who were later called Children of Israel. This very custom gave concern to Abraham as he viewed God's promise to his progeny. Genesis 15:2 reads: "And Abram said, Lord God, what will Thou give me, seeing I go Childless, and the steward of my house is this Eliezer of Damascus?" That the Israelites continued the custom of having a servant become the head of the family when the deceased family head had no son is illustrated in I Chronicles 2:34–35, where it is stated: "Now Sheshan had no sons, but daughters. And Sheshan had a servant, an Egyptian, whose name was Jarha. And Sheshan gave his daughter to Jarha his servant to wife; and she bare him Attai. And Attai begat Nathan, and Nathan begat Zabad . . . ."

We notice that is a servant marrying the family head's daughter, and this servant is an Egyptian. The marginal notes of the Bible dates his succession circa 1471 B.C., and the passage names twelve generations of sons to come from this union. Jarha, the Egyptian servant, must have married Sheshan's daughter before the Exodus journey; thus the Chronicle is able to list such a host of sons and grandsons, many of whom became heads of families in their turn.

There is, we are told, an Asante proverb which says: "A wise slave who knows how to serve succeeds to his master's property."[1] This proverb was absolutely true in pre-colonial Africa, for there are instances when a slave became not only the head of the family, but became king of the nation, as was the case with King Ajaja of Oppobo in what is now a part of Nigeria. The case of Joseph is a prime example to prove that a slave or bought servant was not regarded as being an inferior being. He was well treated as a member of two prominent households, the second of which was the Pharaoh's. The slave boy, who was sold and bought and imprisoned, married the daughter of the priest-prince of On and became Egypt's second-in-power to the king.

The people who were "domestic slaves" or purchased servants were usually people whom circumstances had left without a family. The master of the house gave them his protection, and it is said that among some West African people, the master of the house would fight if someone called his servant a slave. This system of servitude exists in Africa today, and just as in ancient years, the servant is sometimes a relative or an in-law, who not only finds protection from the master, but receives training in the skills of the master.

The African who became a bought servant came to that status sometimes through capture in battle, and sometimes such status came as the result of punishment for crime. Here again the African code and the Mosaic code carry the same provisions, for Exodus 22:2 says: "If a thief be found breaking up, and he be smitten that he die, there shall no blood be shed for him. If the sun be risen upon him, there shall no blood be shed for him; for he should make full restitution; if he have nothing, then he shall be sold for his theft."

As was said before, some people became owned servants by having no near kin to care for them, and in some instances, circumstances of poverty were overcome by one's being sold to a far relative. This same practice was carried on among the Israelites, who by law were forbidden to steal and sell people at all. (During the Atlantic slave trade, many Jews forgot the injunction against selling people.) The Israelites were permitted, however, to buy servants even among fellow Israelites. According to Exodus 21:7, a man could actually sell his daughter to be a maid servant. However, there was no such thing in Israel or in Africa as slavery or servanthood *durante vita* (for life), no was there ever heard of anything like perpetual slavery, wherein a man is a slave before he is born because his parents were enslaved. In Israel the owned servant went free after six years. Ownership of a person carried the obligation to feed, shelter, and clothe him. There will be more said on this question of servitude later, because the practice no doubt contributed to the phenomenal enlargement of the Israelite population, but it must be pointed out that neither in Africa nor in Israel could it ever have been said that servanthood made up the majority of the population—not nearly so.

When Joseph was carried into the land of the black presence, he left behind him a multi-ethnic family—a family that was already racially mixed by intermarriage and plurality of wives. This factor of racially mixing of the family is an important element in determining the reasons for the tremendous growth of the Israelites in so short a time, and someday a competent study of given and surnames in Israel will lead to a more nearly exact account of the mixture.

Jacob had broken with some of the traditions and precedents established by his father Isaac and his grandfather Abraham. He acted differently from Abraham when he kept all of his sons with him as one family and gave to each son a proper inheritance and his right to a proper heritage. Abraham sent away his first, and for thirteen years, his only son Ishmael, whose mother was an Egyptian servant. The Bible says that Abraham had God's approval for his actions, but many of us who revere him wish that he had acted differently before he asked God's approval. The picture of a helpless and sincere woman, ousted from her only home and household, wandering around in the wilderness with a child dying of thirst does not inspire admiration for Abraham's character. When we call Abraham "the father of the faithful," many of us wish that the picture of wandering Hagar and thirsty Ishmael were not there. At a later date Abraham also sent away the six sons, seven grandsons, and three great-grandsons born to him by his wife Keturah, whom he married following Sarah's death. Genesis 25:4–5 says: "And Abraham gave all that he had unto Isaac. But unto the sons of the concubines, which Abraham had, Abraham gave gifts, and sent them away from Isaac his son, while he yet lived, eastward, unto the East Country." These people are said to be a part of the heritage of the Midianites and the Amalekites.

Jacob kept all of his sons, regardless of who the mothers were. His seed was his seed, and herein he first broke with the family tradition. Dan, Naphtali, Gad, and Asher were born to Jacob by Bilhah and Zilpah, women who were given as maids to Jacob's two wives by their father Laban. The boys took great pride in their family, and the evidence is found in their answer to the great Egyptian governor, Zaphnathpaaneah, when he suggested that they were spies at work in Egypt. They did not realize that he was their long-separated brother, and answering his accusation they replied, "We are all one man's sons." (Gen. 42:11)

Jacob kept all his sons together, and most likely never knew that some ill will existed among them for a while. The ill will existed between Joseph and the four sons of Bilhah and Zilpah, and it was engendered when the seventeen-year-old Joseph rendered to the father a bad report against them (Gen. 37:2). It might have been that this "evil report" was the real cause of Joseph's being sold into slavery, for it hardly seems that a father's love for the baby son, and a lad's dream of self-glory could of themselves engender such hatred in the hearts of a man's own brothers as to sell him into slavery.

Jacob also broke a family precedent in not sending his sons to marry their cousins in Padanaram, no did he ask for any of his cousins to be brought into Canaan to wed any of his sons. Abraham, who was married to his half-sister, sent his trusted steward, Eliezer of Damascus, to bring back his niece Rebekah (Rebecca) to wed Isaac. This is one of the beautiful love stories of the Bible, for both these young people seemingly fell in love at first sight. Jacob himself had been sent to Padanaram to live with and labor for his uncle Laban. According to family wish, he married twice in Laban's family: he took both Leah and Rachael.

But Jacob's sons were too young to marry when he brought his family out of Padanaram. The oldest boy could not have been more than thirteen years of age, because his father had worked seven years before his first marriage. Furthermore, Jacob perhaps would not have thought of sending back for wives for his sons, because there had been resentment between the two families. Jacob and Laban made a truce, or effected a reconciliation, around the stone pillar in Mt. Gilead and invoked the Mizpah to make sure of their good faith, but the sons of Laban disliked Jacob, for they had been heard to say: "Jacob hath taken away all that was our father's; and of that which was our father's hath he gotten all his glory." (Gen. 31:1) It would not have been wise for Jacob to have sent his sons to live and bargain surrounded by such a sentiment that was permeated with such hostility.

Another difference between Jacob and his fathers is noted in Jacob's attitude towards the wives that his sons chose and would choose. He had no objections against them on any ground of their place of origin. Old and feeble Abraham had required his oldest servant to place a hand beneath Abraham's thigh and swear by the Lord God of heaven and earth that he would not take a Canaanite wife for Isaac. Instead he was required to go back to Mesopotamia and select Isaac's wife from among Isaac's own kinfolk. The steward wanted to be clear in his mind as to the next step in case his mission failed, and so he asked Abraham what should be done in case no kinswoman would come to wed Isaac. Abraham emphatically stipulated that in the event no kinswoman would come to wed his son, then Isaac was to be taken to his father's homeland in Mesopotamia, and never again brought back to Canaan.

It is recorded that both Isaac and Rebekah in their turn became bitter in spirit when their forty-year-old son Esau went and married two Hittite women. It was for this very reason that Rebekah connived with Jacob to steal from Esau the right of the firstborn, which right not only included the headship of the family but gave one-half of a man's estate to the firstborn. Isaac was old and partially blind and perhaps might have been reconciled to Esau's wedding choices, but it was Rebekah who said that life would not do her any good if her son Jacob should marry any of the daughters of Heth, or someone from the land around them. The old couple acted in secrecy in sending Jacob to Padanaram with instructions to marry among his cousins. Esau discovered the unhappiness of his parents because of his choices in marriage, and he sought to atone for what he had done by marrying yet a daughter of Ishmael. He hoped desperately to win back lost parental favor by his third marriage, but alas the die was cast. His parents would not be reconciled to his wives and family.

Jacob had a different attitude towards the wives and children of his sons. He disregarded all matters pertaining to ethnic, racial, or national origin or family background. Jacob not only accepted the wives which they chose, but he also claimed their offspring to be his own. He would have it understood, "These are my Sons."

The record discloses that both Judah and Simeon married Canaanite women, and both families were well accepted by Jacob as his own. Furthermore, Jacob accepted into his family all the children and wives from the household of the deceased prince of the Hittites, Shechem. His son Hamor had raped Jacob's daughter Diana, after which the prince sought to join his son Hamor in wedlock to her. Jacob's sons consented to the marriage with the stipulation that prior to marriage all the men in Shechem's household would undergo circumcision, and to this they agreed. The operations were performed, and during the days of soreness and illness therefrom, Simeon and Levi, the father of the priestly tribe, killed every male in Shechem's household, including Shechem and his son Hamor. It was their determination that their sister would not be mistreated by any rapist who remained alive. Jacob was thoroughly shaken by the rash actions of his sons, and he very much feared some retaliation from his neighbors; thus, he took his entire family back to Bethel where he had in a vision once seen God standing above a ladder that reached from earth to heaven, with holy angels ascending and descending the ladder. It was here that he built El Bethel (the house of God) and again heard God's promise that a nation would come from his loins, and during this worship period, all the women in the family of the deceased Hittite named Hamer were now members of Jacob's family group.

Jacob's family included wives, maid-concubines, all his sons and daughters, daughters-in-law of whatever ethnic origin, the Hittite females from the household of Shechem. Finally, he discovered that his son Joseph had married an Egyptian girl and had sired two sons. Jacob had Joseph bring the boys to his bedside, where he laid hands upon each and, by right of being head of the family, announced to Joseph that Ephraim and Manasseh were his; and a new era was born for the Israelites. Jacob's family outgrew the families of his father's not because he had many more sons—Abraham himself had eight—but because he honored his own blood whatever it engendered. He suffered from no bigotry, and therefore a son was a son, and a daughter-in-law was a daughter, and a grandchild was also a son. Here lies the beginning of the group called "the Children of Israel." As they were then, so they continued to be throughout the Egyptian sojourn.

Both polygyny and intermarriage with non-Hebrew people were very potent factors supporting the growth of the Israelite nation. It had already been established that the children of plural wife marriages were treated with equal regard after Isaac's time, and the Mosaic law protected the rights of the firstborn—even if his mother had been the father's wife that was hated (Deut. 21:15–17). Many people have grossly misunderstood the Mosaic injunction against marrying people of other ethnic and religious groups. Actually the Mosaic law did frown upon intermarriage with the Canaanites, because the latter were regarded as being corrupted by their own moral customs and capable of converting the Israelites to their form of idol worship. But the law, while frowning upon certain marriages, yet made provisions by which marriages could be effected with women of other groups, even if they were considered enemy groups. The twentieth chapter of Deuteronomy commands Israel to destroy utterly every breathing entity among the various people of Canaan, but the same chapter issues different instructions concerning the people living in cities that were "far off" from them at a given time. In the latter-type conquests, they were directed to keep the women and children along with other usable spoils. Deuteronomy 21:11 goes so far as the following instructions: "And seest among the Captives a beautiful woman, and hast a desire unto her, that thou wouldst have her to wife; then thou shalt bring her home to thy house; and she shall shave her head, and pare her nails; and she shall put the raiment of her captivity from off her, and shall remain in thine house, and bewail her father and her mother a full month; and after that thou shalt go in unto her, and be her husband, and she shall be thy wife."

The Israelites continued their post-Isaac custom of taking foreign women into their families and nation, and they constantly married Canaanite women with the consent of and sometimes in spite of the Mosaic law prohibiting some of these marriages. Even as late as the Babylonian-Persian exile, Ezra the Priest returned to devastated Jerusalem and forced the men of the remnant to get rid of their foreign wives and the children of such unions. As the opposite of Ezra's latter-day action, an incident is illustrative: During the wilderness sojourn, the Israelites won a battle against a coalition of five Midianite kings. They deliberately slaughtered all the men and boys found in the nations of their enemies, and they likewise slew all the women who had experienced sexual intercourse; but they kept for themselves, and added to their families, every female that had retained vaginal chastity, thus continuing to add non-Hebrew people to the nation as they did in Egypt—and in fact as they had since the beginning of Jacob's leadership.

Throughout her post-Isaac history, various people and

personalities of Israel contracted marriages with foreign people. Moses, for example, married the Ethiopian Zipporah. Boaz married Ruth the Moabitess. David married the daughter of a Geshurite king, and he also married Beersheba the Hittite, who bore Solomon and three other sons. Solomon in turn married many foreign or strange women (I Kings 11:1), including the Canaanite woman who bore Rehoboam, later to be king in Solomon's stead. David's sister Abigail was the wife of Jether the Ishmaelite, and the famous architect and designer Hiram of Tyre was the son of a Israelite woman and a man of Tyre.

With the exceptions of Joseph, the woman whose son was executed in the wilderness, and Sheshan's daughter, there are not too many instances wherein it was pointed out that an Egyptian admixture was involved, and in the cases that are cited, there were special reasons for the fact that the chroniclers took time to make such explanations; but we must remember that he was writing for people who already knew the facts involved. He did not need to tell them what they all knew officially and by custom and sight. Considering the presence of such a large Exodus population and the marriage situation among Jacob's sons and their sons' sons, along with the built-in provisions of the Mosaic code and other customs in Israel, it becomes clear that a high amount of intermarriage took place during the Egyptian sojourn. The overwhelming portion of their neighbors were Egyptians, living with large numbers of Libyans and Cushites and some other Asians. The Israelites were already mixed in such a way as to make bigotry impossible. They could hold no prejudice towards color or national origin. The fact that they saw so many black people was not even something to notice or write about; it was to them, no doubt, a natural scene. At times the chroniclers designated people by their countries or national groups, but they never find occasion to say that a certain man was black or brown, or tan or yellowish. Such color designations were unnecessary except in rare instances, and the people knew all about it. Common sense tells us that if Absalom was black (and it is generally known that he was), then there must have been some black either in David or in Maachah the Geshurite, who was Absalom's mother. If the speaker in the Book of Proverbs who calls attention to the fact that she was "black and beautiful"[2] was an Israelite, then it stands to reason that there was black either in her father or in her mother. The fact that the Israelites took color in stride signifies that they must have been very accustomed to it, and until this day no one is able to say which biblical character was black and which was not. Solomon got along very well with the Queen of Sheba, and Jeroboam eagerly sought and found political asylum with Shishak of Egypt. It might have been that the streets of Israelite cities ran the same range of color as do the streets of Middle Eastern cities today. The children of Israel that Moses led would, beyond all doubt, feel strangely different in Hershey, Pennsylvania; but the facts lead to the belief that they would not feel nearly so obvious in Harlem in New York City.

As we turn our attention to other points concerning the pre-Exodus Israelites, we note that studies dealing with their sojourn in Egypt invariably place all of the emphases upon the bad days of suffering. They emphasize the bondage, the lash, the forced labor, and the genocide, and much understanding has been lost by the almost complete exclusion of the better days; it is a study of these better days that helps us to know these people better.

It is very obvious that the Children of Israel saw some very bad years in Egypt, but it is equally as obvious that all of their years in Egypt were not filled with bondage and suffering. A close and thoughtful study of the period shows that the Israelites experienced some of the best, if not their best years in Egypt, and there is difficulty in trying to determine if the good years did not last longer than the bad ones.

During the lifetime of Joseph, his influence never waned, and the fortune of his people did not change. He entered Egypt as a slave at the tender age of seventeen years, but he became governor at the early age of thirty and died at the ripe old age of one hundred ten years; thus his personal presence and his influence held sway in Egypt for eighty years. The last paragraph of the Book of Genesis says: "And Joseph saw Ephraim's children of the third generation; The children also of Machir the son of Manasseh were brought up upon Joseph's knees." The two verses recorded immediately before the beginning of the Exodus narrative which tells us of Israel's downfall portray to us a long and fruitful period. Exodus 1:6, 7 reads, "And Joseph died, and all his brethren, and all that generation. And the children of Israel were fruitful, and increased abundantly, and multiplied, and waxed exceeding mighty; and the land was filled with them." It is following this revelation that the narrative begins to deal with the dark days under the reign of "The New King that knew not Joseph."

The term "mighty," when used to describe a group of Old Testament people, refers to the strength of numbers. This is almost invariably true when it is applied to groups or nations, and here we find a group of people impressive enough in numbers to merit the description "mighty" following the death of Joseph—just eighty-plus years after one family had taken up residence in the land of Egypt. But there is an earlier indication of Israel's phenomenal expansion. The growth of the Israelites was worthy of note in the sojourn story before the death of Jacob is reported. We know from the Scripture that Jacob lived in the land of Egypt only seventeen years, and still Genesis 47:27 can say, "And Israel dwelt in the land of Egypt, in the country of Goshen; and they had possessions therein, and grew, and multiplied exceedingly." Judging from the size of the multitude that went to Canaan to bury Jacob, the Israelites had already become a large and important segment in their new land. It is significant that the Egyptians mourned for Jacob seventy days, and it is also revealing to learn that the whole family could make the trip to Canaan because they could leave their flocks, their herds, and their children in the hands of someone—presumably in the care of servants and hired people.

We must take the time to study the social situation in Egypt during the Hebrew stay if we are to find a satisfactory explanation of Israel's speedy and unnatural growth in that land. Many factors must be taken into consideration.

When Jacob and his family first moved into Egypt, they found a native population that were landless, without civil rights, without opportunities for independent action, and permanently tied to whatever particular area of land upon which they worked and lived by order of the Pharaoh, who literally owned both the people and the land. The very plan through which the king had acquired ownership of land and people was propounded and executed by Joseph, the Hebrew, who used the unfortunate conditions of a seven-year famine to bring the people to their knees in submitting to Pharaoh's ownership. When Joseph's plan had been completely carried out, Pharaoh was the sole owner of the land and the people, and he was therefore able to move the people around at will. First the former landowners were ordered to move to the cities, and from thence they were assigned by Pharaoh to work certain designated portions of land. They were given seed by the king and told that they could live on and work the land, but one-fifth of all the produce was to belong to the king.

It would be foolish to think that the native-stock Egyptian people ever forgot who it was that authored and carried out such widespread evictions and subjugations. This alone would cause the people to wish for the day when they could regain their freedom and their country from the cruel domination of the Hyksos conquerors and their Hebrew allies. There must have been a seething hatred for the Israelites that kept itself alive with underground messages (oral or written) and plans for overcoming someday. The Egyptian grudge against the Hebrew Joseph and his following was surely born when this occurred, and it probably grew as the Hebrews received more and more favorable treatment from the enemy kings.

According to the Bible, the land of the "priests" was not taken over by Pharaoh, and this term "priest" is also translated as "prince." These prince-priests would have been the rulers of the monarchies that historians tell us came into existence after the end of the Old Kingdom, which fell into ruins about 2475 B.C. These monarchy rulers seized the opportunity to establish themselves in the intermediate period of confusion before the monarchy was restored. Their lands and estates became inviolable possessions, held by the right of inheritance and protected by private armies. No king could ascend the throne and rule without reckoning with them, and whatever centralized armies there were had to be supported by the private armies of these nobles, for they could not be overcome. Pharaonic rule had been securely reestablished by 2160 B.C., but "in the end pharoanic rule was restored only by accepting the hereditary rights of the monarchs and allowing them to retain a measure of their power."[3]

These feudal monarchs held their individual power and place during the prosperous days of the Middle Kingdom, and continued to hold sway during the reign of the Asian Hyksos kings. They remained in power until the Thebans defeated the Hyksos, driving the latter out of Egypt and into such obscurity that they cannot be positively identified today. Some of the feudal monarchs of middle and lower Egypt had been allies and supporters of the Hyksos tyrants, and were defeated in war along with the Asian kings. These Thebans, who defeated the aliens and took the throne of Egypt and who simultaneously crushed the power of the monarchs, were the kings that looked upon the descendants of Joseph as enemies, potential and real.

When the history that is reflected in the final chapters of the Book of Genesis is compared to the general history of Egypt, it becomes clear as crystal that Jacob and his sons became feudal monarchs literally overnight. They were made feudal monarchs by Pharaoh's fiat, and their fiefdoms were large, populous, and rich in fertility. They were given "possessions" in Goshen, which Joseph called the best land in Egypt. They were given land at a time when only the feudal priest-princes and the Pharaoh himself owned land. They were not made hirelings to care for Pharaoh's cattle, but they were made "rulers" over those cattle; and the whole cattle country was free from encroachment because the Egyptians shunned "shepherds"—and under the Genesis meaning the term "shepherd" meant herdsman. (Incidentally, the Hyksos are called "shepherd kings," and someone must tell us if the term "shepherd" as found in Genesis also relates to them.) According to the advice of Joseph, every shepherd was "an abomination" to the Egyptians. By his generous gift, the Pharaoh made Jacob and his sons the feudal owners of Goshen, and that carried with it the people who were already tied to the land under Pharaoh's law. From this time forward, the serfs that were already in Goshen had to become servants of the Hebrews. The custom of ownership of children born to servants was later written down by Moses, but as far back as Abraham's time, the term "born in my house" was a statement of ownership; so it must have been that during their stay in Goshen, the children of the servants became the children of the Israelites. This rule held in later Israel even when a Hebrew purchased a fellow Hebrew servant. He remained in servitude only unto the seventh year, but if his wife had been given to him by the master, then the wife and the children continued to belong to the master and were still part of his household.

In the Old Testament world, both bought and hired servants were basic to the economy. There was very little independent labor that could find jobs and change jobs at will. There was practically no middle class, but a two-dimensional society of the "haves and have nots." It was an agrarian society, and tillage depended very largely upon the supply of lands in the household. Even in captivity and dispersal, the children of Israel had bought servants, and the evidence for this assertion is found in the return of many Diaspora Jews in the time of Ezra. The Book of Ezra (2:64–5) gives the following in stating the number of Jews who followed Zerubbabel back to Jerusalem: "The whole congregation together was forty and two thousand three hundred and three score. Beside their servants and their maids, of whom there were seven thousand three hundred and thirty and seven." Here we note that with the Israelites under a captivity that was first brutal and later turned benevolent, the ratio of servants was seven thousand to forty-two thousand. Under these conditions, approximately one-sixth of the returnees were in the status of servants. When the Babylonian captivity is compared to the Egyptian migration, the favorableness of the latter is far more evident, and it would seem that the acquisition of servants and household members would make for a different ratio.

The terms "Hebrew" and "Children of Israel" had different meanings and references. The Hebrew was the genetic descendant of Jacob; "the Children of Israel" included Jacob's genetic descendants and all the Egyptian serfs and servants placed under their ownership by Pharaoh's gift. By the time that the native-stock kings wrested themselves from the grasp of the Hyksos, all outside and other family ties of the serfs and servants in Goshen would have been erased, and there could have been no one else to which they could claim relationship except the families of Jacob. By that time, and after the passing of so many years, they would actually be and would see themselves as "the Children of Israel." The Hebrews were the leaders of this vast horde. They were the lords of the manors, but they and the people were inextricably bound together as a nation. For this reason, perhaps, we always read of "the Children of Israel," but at the same time it is always "the God of the Hebrews." This also possibly accounts for the fact that in every instance, the Scriptures carry very short genealogical lists to cover a nation of millions.

The idea of a two-tiered structure of the Israelite society in Egypt is further bolstered by the account of Pharaoh's vain attempt to induce the midwives to destroy the infant sons of Hebrew women. We notice that only two midwives are said to have been attending the Hebrew women, Shiprah and Puah (Exod. 1:15), and both of them disobeyed Pharaoh's wish to have the Hebrew infants destroyed. In the view of the Abington Commentary and the Dartmouth Bible, the use of only two names for midwives is evidence that the Hebrew community "cannot have been very large," so it should be clearly seen that Pharaoh was seeking to destroy, or to limit, the growth of the Hebrew leadership among the Children of Israel. When this plan failed, "Pharaoh charged all his people saying every son that is born ye shall cast into the river." The term "his people," when spoken about Pharaoh, could mean Egyptians, and thus indicate that the king first sought to destroy Israel's leadership potentialities; then failing in this, he enlarged his plan in order to induce native-stock servants to destroy Israel's soldier potentialities. Pharaoh's reference to the sons of Hebrews could point to the upper tier of Israel's society in Egypt, and the charge to "his people" could point to the lower tier.

During the latter half of Israel's sojourn in Egypt, there was intense suffering indeed. The rise of the "New King over Egypt" initiated an era of fierce persecution for the children of Israel. A conquered people had thrust off the foreign yoke, and naturally they were hostile towards the people whom they regarded as collaborators, allies, friends, or favorites of their deposed oppressors. We have said that it is likely that they never forgot what Joseph did to them. The native-stock Pharaoh knew that Israel wanted to leave, and he appears to have suspected that Israel's armies would make common cause with any Asian enemy who engaged in war with Egypt; and from the facts at hand, it does seem that the tribes of Israel had their private armies. We must take into account the historians who tell us that private armies were maintained by monarchies from the days of the Middle Kingdom. Added to this are the scriptural references to Israel's armies in such passages as Exod. 6:26, 7:4, 12:51. The greatest indication of all is seen in the fact that Moses never trained any armies. He did organize the national army, but we find no record of any training in soldiery nor in weaponry; yet within less than three months after they left Egypt, the "swordsmen" of Israel won a battle against the desert-hardened forces of Amalek at Rephidim (Exod. 17:8). Israel's assault was led by young Joshua, who selected the men (of whom he had to have prior knowledge) with whom he "discomfited Amalek and his people with the edge of the sword." We are afterwards left to wonder if these swordsmen of Israel remained neutral during the fierce war between the Thebans and Israel's benefactors, the Hyksos. We know that some of the monarchies of middle and lower Egypt did actually fight by the side of the Hyksos, and it is very difficult to believe that the Children of Israel would sit idly by and see the smashing defeat and dethronement of a line of kings to whom they owed everything and upon whom they utterly depended. Such a belief would signify a cowardliness that would be uncharacteristic of the Hebrews and the Israelites in general. Abraham was a fighter and Jacob's sons were fighters; the wilderness journey shows the children of Israel to have been fighters; and finally, the invasion of Palestine was one of the world's grand examples of fighting. So it is too much to ask students of the Bible to believe that the armies of Israel, being six hundred thousand strong, sat in cowardly neutrality while their best friends were overpowered, knowing full well that they would appear to the victors as "an abomination." The huge armies and their past activities could have been the reason that the native-stock Pharaoh spoke with such certainty that the Israelites would be on the side of Egypt's enemies in case of war. In the name of national security, he set out to reduce the Israelites to a broken work force. He placed "taskmasters" over the leaders of Israel and empowered them to use the whip and the lash upon the leaders (note), not upon the people. Israel could no longer choose their own officers. These were chosen by Pharaoh's taskmasters, the ones that applied the lash to them when the daily tasks were not fulfilled.

The closing pages of this chapter turn attention to the family of Moses. Moses was Israel's lawgiver and greatest leader. He had an Egyptian name which he never changed, and he married into a black family in the land of Midian. He was the father of two sons, Gershom and Eliezer. The color or nationality of Zipporah is mentioned in Numbers 12:1, where it is recorded that Miriam and Aaron, sister and brother of Moses, spoke against the marriage of Moses. The reference does not say that they murmured against his being married to Zipporah, but they spoke against him because of her.

Several scholars apparently are reluctant to accept the designation of "Ethiopian" as pertaining to Zipporah, because she was a Midianite, and by some stretch of logic these scholars call the Midianites "Arabians." But according to Genesis, these Midianites are the descendants of other than Arabians. The Arabian-theory scholars mean to point out that the Midianites were the descendants of Abraham and Keturah and therefore could not have been black. This logic has led some people to conclude that probably Zipporah had died and Miriam and Aaron were murmuring against Moses's choice of a second wife.

Judging from direct biblical references, either the Midianites as a whole were black people, or there were definitely black tribes and individuals among them. This is most prominently borne out by the biblical passage that calls the wife of Moses an Ethiopian woman, for the marginal notes refer to his marriage to the daughter of Jethroe; we know that the Greeks would only have made such translation for "burnt-faced people," and the King James scholars only used it instead of Cush. The theory of black in Midian is also supported by the Habakkuk statement (Hab. 3:7) that he "saw the tents of Cushan in affliction; and the curtains of the Land of Midian did tremble"; and, as stated elsewhere, the Habakkuk reference traces back to Judges 3:8, where we meet Cushan-rish a thaim, king of Mesopotamia.

The black people of the Old Testament world were not confined to Egypt and Cush, however. References have traced them to various parts of Asia, including the Caspian area and India, where Herodotus saw "the same tint of skin, which approaches that of the Ethiopians." In the account of the sale of

Joseph, the terms "Ishmaelites" and "Midianites" are used interchangeably.

We who have been victims of Western and especially American racism, often find it difficult to understand a world wherein no stigma is attached to a black skin; a world wherein a Hebrew conceived of himself as a descendant of Noah's son Shem, and simultaneously declared that black Africans were descendants of Noah's grandson Cush.

It is certain that Miriam and Aaron did not speak against Zipporah because of her color. They were more than familiar with black people, for they were both born and reared in Egypt, and they were daily surrounded by black kinfolk. Under the circumstances though, they could be expected to have complained against Zipporah's aloofness. She was just not one of them and she never became one of them. She was an exalted princess, a citizen of a landed and stable permanent society, and they were a homeless people drifting towards someplace of which she had never before heard. She had not liked what appeared to her to be the barbaric custom that Moses called circumcision, and if she ever took any part of their society no one bothered to mention it. Some members of Jethroe's family accompanied Moses and the Children of Israel, but maintained their separate identity for many centuries. They were principally known as Kenites, and acknowledged to be descended from the priest-prince to whom Moses deferred and treated with respect and honor. Jethroe is variously called Revel (Exod. 2:18), Jethro (Exod. 3:1), Raguel (Num. 10:29) and Jether (Exod. 2:18, margin).

Hobab, who seems to have been Zipporah's brother, was finally persuaded by Moses to be their guide or scout (Num. 10:29–31). According to promise, the Kenite family was given land in Canaan. Their possession was within the boundaries of Judah's inheritance. They lived in the "wilderness of Judah" (Judges 1:16), where they dwelt in tents and lived the traditional life of nomads until the destruction of Judah in Jeremiah's day. These Kenites were highly respected by the Israelites and their kings. King Saul had allowed them to move away from among the Amalekites before he unleashed his military onslaught that conquered from Havilah to the borders of Egypt (I Sam. 30:29). King Saul remembered their service in the wilderness and saved them, he said, because "Ye showed kindness to all the Children of Israel, when they came out of Egypt." That the original nation of Kenites were Israel's enemies is mysteriously suggested in Balaam's Curse (Num. 24:21), but the in-laws of Moses remained under the protection of Israel for the lifetime of the Israelite nation. The woman who killed Sisera of Harosheth, captain of the armies of Jabin, king of Canaan (Judges 4:17) was a descendant of Moses' in-laws. Deborah the prophetess sang of her: "Blessed above women shall Jael the wife of Heber the Kenite be, blessed shall she be above women in the tent." And in I Chronicles 2:55, the Kenites are mentioned as scribes.

Zipporah's aloofness and apartness is exemplified by the conduct of her family descendants as told in the prophecy of Jeremiah (35:). The prophet used them to teach Judah the unlearned lesson of faithfulness to God and tradition, so following instructions from God, Jeremiah brought the entire household of the Rechabites (Kenite descendants—see marginal note and trace) into the temple chamber of the princess. He set before them pots of wine with cups and ordered them to drink. They refused, saying that their ancestor, Jonadab, had forbidden them to drink wine forever. They went further to explain that they had continued to follow the family patriarchs legacy of life-style as desert nomads; that they had built no permanent houses nor had they planted any seeds or vineyards. They said that they had come to Jerusalem only because they were fleeing before the army of Nebuchadrezzar. Jeremiah said the Lord God of Israel would guarantee the survival of these Kenites, "Because Ye have obeyed the commandment of Jonadab, your father, and kept all his precepts, and done according unto all that he hath commanded you." The prophet said that Judah had done just the opposite and that therefore evil would be brought against them.

There is no record in Scripture of an inheritance of Moses, nor to his sons. Perhaps Gershom and Eliezer and their mother remained in Midian or returned there following the death of Moses.[4] Everybody else among the Children of Israel was given an inheritance, and most of them are recorded. Moses' only inheritance in the land towards which he led Israel comes through his black in-laws, who remained separate and apart. They disappear from record when Jerusalem was destroyed by the Babylonians.

Questions

1. What belief sustained the Israelites during the Egyptian bondage?
2. Where were the Hebrews first called "the Children of Israel?"
3. What type of slavery did Joseph experience?
4. From whence came the concept of chattel slavery?
5. Can you cite biblical proof that Israelite fathers who had no sons gave their daughters in marriage to servants to continue the family line?
6. What facts show that Jacob's family was multi-ethnic?
7. Why did Isaac and Rebecca become bitter towards Esau?
8. Were Israelites permitted to marry non-Israelite people?
9. How did the Hebrews become feudal lords in Egypt?
10. How old was Joseph when he died?
11. Explain the Old Testament passage which says, "Now there arose up a New King over Egypt, which knew not Joseph."
12. What color was the wife of Moses? What was her name?
13. How many sons did Moses have?
14. Did the descendants of Hobab ever become Israelites?

Notes

1. *Ibid.*
2. The Song of Solomon 1:15.
3. *Ibid.*
4. Levitical Priests. I Chronicles 23:14.

8

THE BLACK WARRIOR

MANKIND HAS ALWAYS prayed for peace, while glorifying the warrior at the same time. The pages of history are filled with the noise and din of battle and the crash of arms. Not only has this been true in the secular world as we call it; this has been equally true in the religious world as well, for the Holy Bible itself is crammed full of marching armies. The Old Testament world was like our own in the areas of armed conflict. There were political wars, territorial wars, trade and business wars, and wars fought over causes that were unnamed. There were wars of revenge; wars aimed at broadening the scope of national security; wars fought in order to gain allies; wars to build alliances; wars for imperialism and wars against imperialists; and finally, wars were fought purely on religious grounds. The Old Testament world was full of armed conflict, and the black warrior was there doing his full share of the bloodletting. Along with the others, he fought both offensive and defensive wars; he won some and lost some; he built empires and was sometimes swallowed into empires. The black warrior must have been involved in a great deal of fighting that has not been placed in the record, and this conclusion is supported by the fact that he had gained some reputation for his fighting ability. In a typical burst of prophecy, the fiery Jeremiah (46:9) lists the Cushites (Ethiopians) among "The Mighty Men" of the Egyptian army and reflects that they were infantrymen, for he notes that they "handle the shield."

We have already learned that Egypt began to send her armies into Cush (Kush) prior to about 2200 B.C., and that it was not long after that date that the land of Cush became a part of the Egyptian empire. We can assume that the annexation was not carried out by any peaceful means, and the Cushites must have fought back as best they could. They were at that time not entirely satisfied to be a conquered part of Egypt, and they proved it by reestablishing their independence when the Asian Hyksos captured the throne of Egypt.

As the Cushite country was again taken over by Egypt, there must have been some rather fierce battles fought—even though we do not find any accounts of these battles in the Bible. However, Josephus, the Jewish historian, tells of war between Egypt and Ethiopia (Cush) that was won by the former through an army led by Moses. Other records are silent about this war or series of battles, but Josephus tells the story with apparent certainty concerning his facts, and the best thing to do here is to let Josephus tell the story in his own way:

The Ethiopians, who are next neighbors to the Egyptians, made an inroad into their country, which they seized upon, and carried off the effects of the Egyptians, who, in their rage, fought against them; and revenged the affronts they had received from them; but, being overcome in battle, some of them were slain, and the rest ran away in a shameful manner, and by that means saved themselves; whereupon the Ethiopians followed after them in the pursuit; and thinking that it would be a mark of cowardice if they did not subdue all Egypt, they went on to subdue the rest with greater vehemence; and when they had tasted the sweets of the country, they never left off the prosecution of the war; and as the nearest parts had not courage enough at first to fight with them, they proceeded as far as Memphis, and the Sea itself; while not one of the cities was able to oppose them. The Egyptians, under this sad oppression, betook themselves to the oracles and prophecies; and when God had given them this counsel, to make use of Moses the Hebrew and take his assistance, the King commanded his daughter to produce him, that he might be the General of their army. Upon which, when she had made him swear he would do him no harm, she delivered him to the king, and supposed his assistance would be of great advantage to them. She withal reproached the Priest, who, when they had before admonished the Egyptians to kill him, was not ashamed now to own their want of his help.

So Moses, at the persuasion both of Thermuthis and the King himself, cheerfully undertook the business: and the sacred scribes of both nations were glad; those of the Egyptians, that they should at once overcome their enemies by his valor, and that by the same piece of management Moses would be slain; but those of the Hebrews, that they should escape from the Egyptians, because Moses was to be their General; but Moses prevented the enemies, and took and led his army before those enemies were apprised of his attacking them; for he did not march by the river, but by land, where he gave a wonderful demonstration of his sagacity; for when the ground was difficult to be passed over, because of the multitude of serpents, (which it produces in vast numbers, and indeed is singular in some of those productions, which other countries do not breed, and yet such as ar

worse than others in power and mischief, and an unusual
fierceness of sight, some of which ascend out of the
ground unseen, and also fly in the air, and so come upon
men at unawares, and do them a mischief.) Moses invented a wonderful stratagem to preserve the army safe, and
without hurt; for he made baskets, like unto arks, of sedge,
and filled them with ibes, and carried them along with
them; which animal is the greatest enemy to serpents
imaginable, for they fly from them when they come near
them; and as they fly they are caught and devoured by
them, as if it were done by the harts; but the ibes are tame
creatures, and only enemies to the serpentine kind: but
about these ibes I say no more at present, since the Greeks
themselves are not unacquainted with this sort of bird. As
soon, therefore, as Moses was come to the land which was
the breeder of these serpents, he let loose the ibes, and by
their means repelled the serpentine kind, and used them
for his assistants before the army came upon that ground.
When he had therefore proceeded thus on his journey, he
came upon the Ethiopians before they expected him; and
joining battle with them, he beat them, and deprived them
of the hopes they had of success against the Egyptians,
and went on in overthrowing their cities, and indeed made
a great slaughter of these Ethiopians. Now when the
Egyptian army had once tasted of this prosperous success,
by the means of Moses, they did not slacken their dili-
gence, insomuch that the Ethiopians were in danger of
being reduced to slavery, and all sorts of destruction; and
at length they retired to Saba, which was a royal city of
Ethiopia, which Cambyses afterwards named Meroe, after
the name of his own sister. The place was to be besieged
with very great difficulty. since it was both encompassed
by the Nile quite round, and the other rivers, Astapus and
Astaboras, made it very difficult thing for such as attempted to pass over them; for the city was situate in a retired

place, and was inhabited after the manner of an island, being encompassed with a strong wall, and having the rivers to guard them from their enemies, had having great ramparts between the wall and the rivers, insomuch, that when the waters come with the greatest violence it can never be drowned; which ramparts make it next to impossible for even such as are gotten over the rivers to take the city. However, while Moses was uneasy at the army's lying idle, (for the enemies durst not come to battle,) this accident happened: Tharbis was the daughter of the King of the Ethiopians: she happened to see Moses as he led the army near the walls, and fought with great courage; and admiring the subtlety of his undertakings, and believing him to be the author of the Egyptians' success, when they had before despaired of recovering their liberty, and to be the occasion of the great danger the Ethiopians were in, when they had before boasted of their great achievements, she fell deeply in love with him; and upon the prevalency of that passion, sent to him the most faithful of all her servants to discourse with him about their marriage. He thereupon accepted the offer, on condition she would procure the delivering up of the city; and gave her the assurance of an oath to take her to his wife; and that when he had once taken possession of the city, he would not beak his oath to her. No sooner was the agreement made, but it took effect immediately; and when Moses had cut off the Ethiopians, he gave thanks to God and consummated his marriage, and led the Egyptians back to their own land.[1]

We have read the story in Josephus's own words, and, according to the translator, Irenaeus cites the same incident—having borrowed it from Josephus. We are told no more of Tharbis, nor are we told any more of the wars between Ethiopia and Egypt by Josephus, but the story apparently continued to live, in spite of the fact that nothing like it is mentioned in our Bible. The Italian opera *Aïda* is based upon war between Egypt and Ethiopia, and the plot is different from the story as told by Josephus, but there is a strong similarity between the events. Incidentally, the opera was written by the Italian Giuseppe Verdi in 1871 at the request of Ismail Pasha; it was presented in Cairo, Egypt, in the same year, and, in light of the histories of Egypt and Cush, the story is based upon a war that actually took place. We may need further research and study concerning the love story and its influence on the war, but the actual battles must have taken place at the point in time that is reflected in the history of the countries and the life of Moses. It is a glimpse of some of the earliest recorded activity of the black warrior.

The Josephus account of the war between Cush and Egypt has further value for our study because it gives us some ideas concerning facts that came into the mind of the writer either through history or personal impressions. He calls the country "Ethiopia" but gives the correct location of Cush (Kush). He reveals the presence of a standing army, and, according to his report, an army that boldly and very effectively invaded Egypt-proper, actually on the winning side until Moses took command and pushed them all the way back from the Mediterranean Sea. From some source Josephus finds a name for Pharaoh's daughter, and the name Tharbis for the daughter of the king of Cush. His description of Meroe is very full, especially when it concerns the defensibility of the city—we are told of river protection, of walls and of ramparts. There is no biblical account of the marriage of Moses as told in the narrative under discussion, but in telling us about it, Josephus implies no color problem. The fact that she was black is of no importance to him, and thus it was in the Old Testament world. It is interesting to note that Josephus also tells of the marriage of Moses to Zipporah, the daughter of Jethroe, thus showing that the two marriages were to different women.

Another ancient writer, who is not a biblical one, gives us a glimpse of the black warrior as a part of a marching army. It concerns one of the black components in the Persian army, and although the story is not a biblical story, the Scripture does show that the Persian empire was extensive enough to include the black warrior; this will be mentioned again in Chapter 10. This time our reporter is our old friend Herodotus, who is one of the greatest eyewitness historians of the ancient world. The time herein represented is late in the Old Testament history of the Israelites, but it of interest in this chapter because it is so very descriptive. Herodotus actually saw Ethiopians marching in the Persian army, and under the command of Arsames, son of Darius and Artystone, daughter of King Cyrus, and he described them thus:

> The Ethiopians were clothed in the skins of leopards and lions, and had long bows made of the stem of the palm leaf, not less than four cubits in length. On these they laid short arrows made of reed, and armed at the tip, not with iron, but with a piece of stone, sharpened to a point, of the kind used in engraving seals. They carried likewise spears, the head of which was the sharpened horn of an antelope; and in addition they had knotted clubs. When they went into battle they painted their bodies, half with chalk and half with vermillion.

Behold the black warrior of the Old Testament world, marching into battle in full battle dress in a combat team that included the Arabians, and considered to be of such combat dependability that they were under the command of the emperor's own son. He was truly among the "might men" of the ancient world and Egypt saw him, Israel saw him, Arabia saw him and Greece saw him.

The Book of Judges quite suddenly introduces us to a black warrior who does not come from Cush but from Mesopotamia, and who turned out to be one of the earlier conquerors who afflicted Israel. The story comes from Judges 3:5:

And the Children of Israel dwelt among the Canaanites,
Hittites, and Amorites, and Perrizites, and Hivites and
Jubusites; and they took their daughter to be their wives,
and gave their daughters to their sons, and served other
Gods. And the Children of Israel did evil in the sight of
the Lord, and forgot the Lord their God, and served
Baalim and the groves. Therefore, the anger of the Lord
was hot against Israel, and He sold them into the hand of
Chusan-rishathaim eight years.

The information concerning this particular oppression in the
history of Israel is so very scanty that a full interpretation thereof
is definitely impossible. In fact, the Abington Commentary argues
that the lack of such a great deal of specific detail raises doubts
about the historicity of the entire passage. Many scholars, it is
claimed, doubt that the event ever occurred at all. The Commentary gives no explanation as to why the Book of Judges would
contain such a clear-cut and definite account of an event that
some scholars feel did not actually occur. On the other hand,
Josephus does not treat the story as myth in the least. He draws
from the biblical account the report that Israel had been adverse-
ly affected by her surrounding neighbors; that she had shown
contempt for her own religion, had grown very careless and was
"full of the evil doings of the Canaanites." Josephus also offers
to us some details concerning the conflict that cannot be found
in the Bible story. For example, Josephus says that Israel lost
many soldiers in the war against Cushan-rishathaim, and that the
victor had besieged the country. There was a conquest by force,
of course, but it is said that some of the Israelites submitted
voluntarily.

The conquest of Cushan (Chusan)-rishathaim, whom Josephus
called king of the Assyrians, occurred between 1406 and 1425
B.C., according to biblical account; and Bible students would have
to agree that said period comes too late in Hebrew development
to be purely a myth. Admittedly, the whole affair perhaps

predates the beginning of actually writing the history of the Hebrews, yet by this time the storytellers were well versed in this that was written later. The kingdom of Chusan or Chusan-rishathaim, is designated in biblical text as Mesopotamia, and in the margin as Aram-Naharaim, which some authorities also say points to Mesopotamia, and literally means "highland of or between two rivers."

It is said that the term "Aram" is an area designated by the Hebrews as the country northeast of Palestine and is usually translated as Syria. The earliest occurrence of the term "Aram" comes to us in the form of Aram-Naharaim, and is at that time designated as Mesopotamia. It is further explained by certain scholars that the geographical area under consideration contained a number of smaller powers prior to the hegemony of Damascas, who in time absorbed them all; from thence forward the term "Aram" applies to Damascas alone.

To follow the marginal references and various definitions and references in Bible dictionaries and commentaries leads to greater confusion in trying to determine the facts concerning Israel's oppression under Chusan or Cushan-rishathaim. Some of this confusion, for example, is experienced in reading 2 Samuel 8:1–8. Here we find that King David overcame the Philistines, the Moabites, and that he "smote also Hadeazer (the margin renders it Hadarezer), the son of Rehob, King of Zobah, as he went to recover his border at the river Euphrates." The fifth verse of the same chapter contributes to the account by saying, "And when the Syrians of Damascus came to Succor Hadadezer of Zobah, David slew of the Syrians two and twenty thousand men." This establishes the fact, it seems, that the kingdom of Zobah under Hadadezar was a different power from the kingdom of Syrians of Damascus. Thus this passage appears to give support to the definition of Chusan-rishathaim that is given by the Bible dictionary, which defines the title as meaning "chief of two governments of Mesopotamia—B.C. after 1420."

The pertinency of this entire treatment of the eighth chapter

of Judges is established by the marginal reference, which points
to the third chapter of the prophecy of Habakkuk, the third verse
of which says, "I saw the tents of Cushan in affliction; and the
curtains of the land of Midian did tremble"; and the marginal
note here changes "Cushan" to "Ethiopia," which is the Greek
term designating the land of Cush and literally meaning "burnt
faces." The dictionary of the Bible compiled by William Smith
refers the reader to the third chapter of Judges, saying that the
Chushan-rishathaim herein mentioned is possibly the same
Cushan mentioned in Habakkuk, and the term is defined as
meaning "blackness." The Abingdon Commentary regards the
name Chusan-rishathaim as being a descriptive title rather than
a proper name, but admits that the term literally means "the
Cushite of double wickedness."

After all the information about the third chapter of Judges has
been gathered, studied, defined, sifted, and woven into an
intelligible whole, there are a few points that stand out clearly.
Very definitely at the time between about 1300 and 1000 B.C.,
Israel had a leader identified by the name Othniel, said to have
been nephew to Caleb. His claim to history rests upon the fact
that under his leadership the Israelites arose and threw off the
yoke of a tyrant by the name of Chusan or Chusan-rishathaim.
The tyrant was an imperialist, as proven by the fact that he is
designated by a name meaning "chief of two governments." His
conquests included the area of Assyria, or Mesopotamia, or
Midian, for such area is mentioned in some of the references. His
name also accommodates the title "of double wickedness," which
definitely suggests that his conquests had multiplied before the
conquest of Israel. The final and central point of pertinency is in
finding that the tyrant under study was black. We do not know
how he came to be black, nor how he happened to get into the
Mesopotamia area, but the black part of his identification seems
beyond argument. Whether Chusan or Chusan-rishathaim is a
descriptive title or a proper name, there are no grounds for
doubting that he was a black warrior, and thus for eight years

the Children of Israel were ruled and governed by a man whom later the Europeans would call a "Negro." In 1865, Philip Smith published *The History of the World*, and taking literally the passages Genesis 10:8–10 and 11:1–6, argues that Cushites (descendants of Nimrod) built Babel and dwelt on the lower level of Mesopotamia; this included Babylon by the Euphrates—the home of Chushan-rishathaim.

The next mention of black warriors in the Bible is very clear and unmistakable and does not require a search of marginal notes nor the decisions of Bible dictionaries. This refers to the black soldiers in the army of Shishak, king of Egypt. He is mentioned in the first Book of Kings, but the very pertinent details are set forth in the twelfth chapter of 2 Chronicles:

> And it came to pass, that when Rehoboam had established the kingdom, and had strengthen himself, he forsook the law of the Lord, and all Israel went with him. And it came to pass that in the fifth year of King Rehoboam Shishak King of Egypt came up against Jerusalem, because they had transgressed against the Lord, with twelve hundred chariots, and three score thousand horsemen; and the people were without number that came with him out of Egypt; The Lubims (dwellers in a thirsty land), the Suk-kims, and the *Ethiopians*.

The Shishak that is mentioned here is said to have been Sheshong I of Egypt, the Libyan who was the power that wrested the throne from native-stock kings to form the Twenty-second or Bubastite Dynasty; the first reign lasted from around 950 to 929 B.C. His sister Taphenes was married to an Edomite named Hadad, who had escaped David's army during the Edomite campaign led by Joab. Also the industrious and ambitious young Jeroboam had found refuge with Shishak when he fled from King Solomon who was determined to kill him for planning to lead a revolt in the Hebrew kingdom. After Solomon's death, Jeroboam returned to Israel and rather automatically became king of Israel (the northern kingdom) when the Solomonic Kingdom disintegrated in the hands of Solomon's son, Rehoboam.

Shishak, who was a friend to Jeroboam of Israel, appears to have become an archenemy to Rehoboam of Judah, and just five years after the death of Solomon, he invaded Judah, the southern kingdom. He conquered Judah and all her cities without a fight; even Rehoboam and Jerusalem surrendered peacefully. The victor proceeded to loot and plunder the Temple and its treasury and left Jerusalem carrying all the gold and silver, even the golden shields. Josephus affirms the fact that Judah was under tribute or taxation to this pharaoh. Josephus says that the Shishak army had many charioteers and calvary, and that there were four hundred thousand infantrymen; and declares that the greatest number of Shishak's troops were Libyans and Ethiopians, thus black warriors played an important part in this subjugation of looted and plundered Judah. He did his share of the bloodletting in the Old Testament world.

Like their co-militarists in all ages, the black warriors of the Old Testament could not always accomplish that which they set out to do. They got the better of some battles and the worst of others; they won some wars and were the losers of others; they at times staved off invasions, and at some points others prevented them from invading strange lands. In 2 Chronicles 14:9 there begins an account of an unsuccessful attempt by a black pharaoh of Egypt to invade the country of Judah. In this instance the Bible itself makes known the color and native origin of the would-be conqueror and gives some of the details concerning his ill-fated invasion:

> And there came out against them Zerah the Ethiopian with a host of a thousand thousand, and three hundred chariots, and came unto Mareshah. Then Asa went out against him, and they set the battle in array in the valley of Zephathah at Mareshah. And Asa cried unto the Lord,

and said, Lord it is nothing with thee to help, whether with many, or with them that have no power; help us, O Lord our God; for we rest on thee, and in thy name we go against the multitude. O Lord, thou art God; let not man prevail against thee.

So the Lord smote the Ethiopians before Asa, and before Judah; and the Ethiopians fled. And Asa and the people that were with him pursued them unto Gerar: and the Ethiopians were overthrown, that they could not recover themselves; for they were destroyed before the Lord and before his Host; and they carried away very much spoil.

The battle just described took place around 941 B.C., and it is possible because of the date that some sources believe that Zerah was Osarken I (or Orsakken II) or possibly an Arabian king. One scholarly source makes the untenable assertion that the above story refers to Arabia and not to Cush; but the facts seem definitely to refute any theory or idea that Zerah was an Arabian, and on several grounds. In the first place, the history of that area and that era shows that there could have been no Arabian power that was able to field an army of one million men in 941 B.C., for according to history, the Minagans—the first Arabian kingdom— date from 200 to 650 B.C., but they were not "militaristically minded." The Sabaen kingdom of Southern Arabia arose in 930 B.C., and the Himyarites kingdom of Saba arose circa 115 B.C. In the second place, the theory that Zerah was Arabian would gain no support from the location of his battle with Asa of Judah. It was strictly a southern battle, that came to its end in the Philistine City of Gerar, where both Abraham and Isaac sojourned; and while enroute to Egypt, God advised Isaac to stay in Gerar. He stayed and prospered. Thus the city of Gerar was situated on the southern or shortest route between Judah and Egypt and had been used by travellers of that day and of earlier days. Around the years of 941 B.C., an Arabian conqueror could not have skipped over the powerful Egypt lying in his path to march an amy to Judah, a route that was combat explosive, which fact is told thusly in the Exodus story: "God led them (the Children of Israel) not through the way of the land of the Philistines, although that was near: for God said, lest peradventure the people repent when they see war, and they return to Egypt: but God led the people about, through the way of the Red Sea," and, we might add, by the way of the Arabian area of influence. The final point in the argument highlights the fact that the chroniclers well knew the Arabians circa 941, and it is highly unlikely that such an error would have been made.

Some of the confusion among historians grows out of the fact that a Cushite king was ruling Egypt as early as 941 B.C. We know that the Twenty-fifth Dynasty was line of Cushite kings, but it began around 700 B.C., and we are taught that the Cushite dynasty lasted a little more than one century; the names of a half-dozen known kings of the dynasty would more than fill such a span of time. On the other hand, we have some testimony from Herodotus, who praised the Egyptians for keeping the best records of any people that he knew. He said that the Egyptian records showed that there had been eighteen Ethiopian kings on the Egyptian throne, so we need not be baffled at all by the emergence of a Cushite king at any date after the country was wrested from the dreaded Hyksos.

Wilson's dictionary of the Bible gives us an enlightening description of the battle between Asa and Zerah, and, remembering that Asa's army was one-half the size of the enemy forces, it makes dramatic reading:

> In the fourteenth year of Asa, Zerah the Ethiopian, with a mighty army of a million, invaded his kingdom and advanced unopposed in the field as far as the valley of Zephathah at Maresha. The Egyptian monuments enable us to picture the general disposition of Zerah's army. The chariots formed the first corps in a single or double line;

behind them, massed in phalanxes, were heavy armed troops; probably on the flanks stood archers and horsemen in lighter formations. After a prayer by Asa, his army attacked the Egyptians and defeated them. The chariots, broken by the charge, and with horses made unmanageable by flights of arrows, must have been forced back upon the cumbrous host behind. So complete was the overthrow that the Hebrews could capture and spoil the cities around Gerar, which must have been in alliance with Zerah. The defeat of the Egyptian army is without parallel in the history of the Jews. On no other occasion did an Israelite army meet an army of one of the great powers and defeat it.

Asa's successful defense against Zerah was called to his attention a few years later, and its memory was used to offer severe criticism to his new foreign policy. The seer Hanani[2] found himself stowed away in prison because he criticized King Asa for seeking the help of King Benhadad of Syria against King Baasha of Israel. Hanani called King Asa's actions foolish because he had given up the opportunity of defeating Syria in battle, thereby avoiding any future wars with them. The great and most serious charge against Asa was that he relied upon man in dealing with Syria and Israel and had disregarded the victory that God had given him over the forces of Zerah. Said Hanani, "Were not the Ethiopians and the Lubims a huge host, with very many chariots and horsemen? Yet because thou didst rely on the Lord, He delivered them into thine hand." In other words Hanani is saying that any man who with only the help of God could defeat what was at that point in time the world's biggest army—that was the army of the black warrior—did not need any king's help in defeating anybody else on earth.

Other chapters tell the stories of Khasta, Piankhy and the famed Taharkah. But the last king of Egypt to fight on Judah's soil was not a Cushite, but he had Cushites, the black warriors, in his army; in fact they, along with the Libyans, made up the bulk of his victorious forces. The story is first introduced in the second Book of Kings: "In his days Pharaoh-Nechoh king of Egypt went up against the king of Assyria to the river Euphrates: and King Josiah went against him, and he slew him at Megiddo when he had seen him."

Following the sad and shocking death of the young King Josiah, the people elevated his son Jehoahaz to the throne. He reigned only three peaceful months: "And Pharaoh-Nechoh put him in bands at Riblah in the land of Hamath, that he might not reign in Jerusalem; and put the land to a tribute of an hundred talents of silver, and a talent of gold. And Pharaoh-Nechoh made Eliakim the son of Josiah king in the room of Josiah his father, and turned his name to Jehoiakim, and took Jehoadah away: and he came to Egypt and died there. And Jehoikim gave the silver and gold to Pharaoh."

This account of Josiah's death is given a more detailed treatment in 2 Chronicles 35:20. In this report the Egyptian king sent personal ambassadors to dissuade Josiah from joining the battle. Said he: "What have I to do with thee, thou king of Judah? I come not against thee this day, but against the house wherewith I have war: for God commanded me to make haste: forebear thee from meddling with God, who is with me, that he destroy thee not." Josiah failed to forebear and was killed at Megiddo.

The Pharaoh-Nechoh who killed Josiah was the second king in the Twenty-sixth Dynasty of Egyptian pharaohs, and reigned between 609 and 594 B.C. His reign was both progressive and successful, for it is said that he built the canal linking the Nile to the Red Sea and sent Phoenician sailors to explore the coast of Africa; and this fleet is said to have circumnavigated the entire continent. Nechoh had extended his boundaries to the Euphrates, and since the Assyrian kingdom had been vanquished, Josiah and the Syrian king wanted to prevent any further thrusts into their area by the Egyptians. In the year 604 B.C., Nechoh was defeated at Carchemish by the Babylonian king Nebuchadrezzar, much to the delight of the prophet Jeremiah. It is from him that we lean very definitely that the black warriors fought with Nechoh, for if they were with him at Carchemish, they certainly were with him at Megiddo. The Cushites were there, for Jeremiah intones:

> Come up, ye horses: and rage, Ye chariots;
> And let the Mighty Men come forth.
> The Cushites and the Libyans, that handle the shield;
> And the Lidians that handle and bend the bow.
> For this is the day of The Lord of Hosts, a day of ven-
> geance,
> That He may avenge Him of His adversaries.[3]

The final illustration showing the presence and prevalence of the black warrior in the wars of the Old Testament world is shrouded in mystery. No one seems to be certain about the identity of Gog, of the land of Magog, which sometimes appears to be Magog, the land of Gog; but nevertheless we have testimony that "burnt-faced" soldiers were part of this heterogeneous and motley horde.

There is agreement among written sources that the group referred to were "Scythians," and were so called by the Greeks. Josephus identified them as "Iberians"—inhabitants of the country lying between the Caspian and Euxine seas, now known as the Black Sea. (This would locate them around the Caucasus Mountains.) Some dictionary sources say that their country was adjacent to that of Togomar or Armenia. Still other sources see them as a nomadic tribe that dwelt mostly on the north sides of the Caspian and Black seas (perhaps around the Volga River), with territory stretching from thence indefinitely into inner Asia. It seems that the "Ma" in the Magog might designate a northern locality. We learn that a few scholars have tended to see the subjects of the Bible stories concerning Magog as myths, but some identifications are too factual and definite to support their theories.

All sources agree that the Scythians were a barbaric people, extremely low in points of intelligence and civilization, but they were able to put together a vast army of "horses and horsemen, all of them clothed with all sorts of armor, even a great company with buckles and shields, all of them handling swords." In their number were Persians, Libyans, people of Togomah of Gomer, and Ethiopians or Cushites. According to Ezekiel 38:1-6 they came from their place in the north; Herodotus reports that they defeated the Medes and were masters of Asia twenty-eight years. Psammeticus or Psamtic saved Egypt from a similar invasion, we are told, by persuading them with gifts. Herodotus accused them of spreading ruin by slaughter and plunder. Ezekiel also inveighs against them for attacking peaceful people in order to "take a spoil", to take cattle and goods, and to capture people to be sold in the slave trade.

Their defeat appears to have come directly from God and without the help or intervention of men. What seems to have been an epidemic swept through their forces to bring such sudden and widespread death that one was left to bury the dead. This was done by wayfarers and burial teams. Their name became a symbol in the Old Testament world of rudeness, badness, low quality, degradation, and disease. Paul's Epistle to the Colossians touches the extremes when he exhorts his readers to seek Christ and put on the new man "Where there is neither Greek nor Jew, circumcision nor uncircumcision, barbarian, Scythians, bond nor free; but Christ is all and in all."

In the Old Testament world, the black warrior permeated the whole scene. He fought with the best and he fought with the worst, but he was there, big, black, bold and beautiful.

Questions
1. What prophet mentions "the Mighty Men of Ethiopia"?
2. Were black soldiers ever in the Persian army? If so, who was their commander?

3. Name the black king who conquered the Israelites during the period of the Judges.
4. Were there any black troops in Shishak's army that is mentioned in the Old Testament?
5. What black king brought a million troops to invade Judah? Did he succeed?
6. Who commanded the army that killed Josiah or Judah? Were there any black troops in that army?
7. Were there any black soldiers with Gog of Magog?
8. Who said that Moses led an Egyptian army into Cush?
9. The opera *Aïda* is based upon war between what nations?
10. According to Herodotus, how many Cushite kings were listed in the Egyptian records?

Notes

1. Flavius Josephus, *The Antiquities of the Jews*, Book 4.
2. 2 Chronicles 16:8–10.
3. Jeremiah 46:9.

9

ALLIES AND TRADING PARTNERS

AFRICA HAS ALWAYS BEEN a continent of trade and trading. This is one of the principal characteristics of the general population of Africa, and especially of sub-Saharan Africa, and is carried on extensively by all ethnic groups. This was the underlying cause of the slave trade, both the Muslim and the Atlantic trade, and is indisputable evidence that African societies have had a very long and stable existence. Long before the first European came upon her scene, and longer still before the Portuguese began to probe the two ocean coasts of the African continent, Africans were skilled and well-known participants in world trade; thus it was that the appearance of European slave traders found people already organized and ready for barter because this was their way of life. For more than two thousand years, the trade had consisted of various usable commodities, but when the Europeans manifested an interest in buying people, the African tradesmen were ready to do business in that respect. What trade the Europeans found during the latter part of the fifteenth and early part of the sixteenth century was something that was too ancient to date. It had gone on for millenniums, and the country of Cush in the Eastern Sudan had been very active since ancient times.

Let us be reminded that the Cushite rule of Egypt proper had ended with the Assyrian invasion of 660 B.C. Esarhaddon had been the leader of the victorious Assyrians, whose iron weaponry proved too formidable for the Egyptian opposers. Incidentally, it was this assault that introduced iron weaponry to the African continent. Egypt for one knew iron, for iron daggers have been unearthed during excavations; but iron had not assumed a place in practical living, nor perhaps had been thought of in terms of weaponry. We will recall from the former chapter that Herodotus, the Greek historian, saw a contingent of Cushite soldiers marching in the Persian army two hundred years after the Assyrian victory, and these Cushite soldiers still carried no iron weapons.

The Cushites withdrew from Egypt under the leadership of King Tanwelamani, who did not lead them back home to die in obscurity, but to continue their nationhood and develop as never before. He was a king who had lost his empire, but he retained his country intact. We do not know definitely how far south the Cushite kingdom extended, but some historians believe that its southern borders perhaps reached the cities of Sonnar and Kosti, which are located well beyond the sixth cataract of the Nile River and are many miles south of modern Khartoum. The Cushites diligently applied themselves to the development of their country and did not again seek the throne of Egypt, in spite of the fact that the Assyrians withdrew.

In something less than a century, the kingdom of Cush was faced with an alien intrusion, and this time it was the Persian army that invaded the capital, Napata, somewhere around 591 B.C. But the Cushite kings averted subjugation and destruction by moving the capital southward to the city of Meroe, which reached about 120 miles north of modern Khartoum. The kingdom refused to vanish from the world, and, on the contrary, went on to develop. It became ever more progressive, and in time became a strong and great world power, as we remember Margaret Shinnie's assertation that Cush was the first truly African nation to become a world power. This required the passing of a number of years, but the resources were there, along with the will and knowledge to make use of them. Iron became the greatest asset of the Cushites, and Meroe became the center of mining and smelting and working in iron. In less than three centuries following the Persian invasion of Napata, Meroe had become one of the greatest ironwork centers in the entire world, and the quality of its iron was acknowledged in other countries and other continents.

As we have seen earlier, the Cushite civilization had been tied to Egyptian civilization something less than two thousand years and had taken on many of the traits of Egyptian civilization, including the Egyptian hieroglyphics; but in time, and following the moving of the capitol of Meroe, the Cushites began to purge their civilization of Egyptian cultural characteristics. As has been pointed out, they developed their own script, which has never been translated, and even their religion became indigenous. On their own and developing their own type of civilization, Meroitic Cush went on to reach its zenith.

Six hundred years is a long time for Meroitic Cush to have laster; yet it did, and it depended upon the exportation of its metals. These people are very prominently a part of the scene during the closing days of the Old Testament. The Old Testament does not mention China and Axum (modern Ethiopia), but it does mention Cush, which leads us to believe that she must have been the most wide-ranging mercantile nation in the world at one time. Rome and Greece are mentioned in the Holy Bible, and Cush was more familiar with them than was Israel at one time; and through her trade, nations unknown to each other were yet linked together—the Far East, the Middle East, southeast Asia, northeast Africa and west Africa. They were all familiar with the imports of Cush: elephants, iron products, ebony, slaves, gum, skins, ostrich feathers, arrowheads, pottery, baskets and jewelry.

Old Testament passages display a familiarity with the ancient land of Cush that came not so much through the travels of Israelites, but through the travels of the Cushites. Most of the references are found in the history reflected in the works of various prophets, and some of these references even suggest the types of vessels that could be seen coming to the Israelite lands from Cush. The prophet Isaiah (18:1–2) tells us about diplomatic exchange between the two nations, Cush being the maritime partner. Her ambassadors came across the sea in ships made of bullrushes. These vessels and sailors must have made an impression upon the Israelites, who themselves were never able to develop very much maritime activity of their own. Israel was largely landlocked in those days. King Solomon was the first ruler to engage in the venture of building and organizing a navy, and he made Elion-Geber its headquarters. This was a city located at the Gulf of Aqabah, which emptied into the Red Sea. It is believed that his crafts were ocean-going vessels that sailed to many ports, among which might have been the East Coast of Africa. Solomon's maritime enterprise remained just that, for he was not able to make Israel a maritime nation, not even to the point of training her own seamen. Israel's navy under Solomon was manned by mercenaries hired from Tyre, and although it was a great venture for one king, these activities could never make a nation itself maritime-conscious.

In another spot the prophet Isaiah (45:14) mentions the "merchandise of Ethiopia" and thus indicates Israel's familiarity with the products of Cush and with the productivity of the Cushites. Ezekiel (30:9) foresaw the day when God would reverse the exchange and "messengers" would take ships to carry fearful tidings to the Cushite people. A very enlightening reference comes from the Book of Job, and it comes through in one of his speeches glorifying wisdom. He labors to show that wisdom is something that comes directly from God, which implies that a man does not attain it, but that he receives it. It is a very valuable and precious thing indeed, exceeding the value of money or any other item of exchange, no matter how dear, expensive, or sought-after such item may be.

> But where shall wisdom be found? And where is the place of understanding? Man knoweth not the price thereof; neither is it found in the land of the living. The depth saith, it is not with me: and the sea saith, it is not with me. It cannot be gotten for gold, neither shall silver be weighed for the price thereof. It cannot be valued with the gold of Ophir, with the precious onyx, or the sapphire. The gold and the crystal cannot equal it: and the exchange of it shall not be for jewels of fine gold. No mention shall be made of coral, or of pearls; for the price of wisdom is above rubies. The topaz of Ethiopia shall not equal it, neither shall it be valued with pure gold. (Job 28:12–19)

Job does not attempt to explain the topaz nor to comment further upon its origin, and this in itself indicates that his hearers must have been as knowledgeable about it as he was. This item was one of the exports of the land of Cush, and was unique in its beauty and usefulness; thus Job cannot illustrate his point merely by mentioning the topaz, for that, no doubt, would not show the exalted place of wisdom. So he goes further and mentions "the topaz of Ethiopia," which was in itself a noted jewel with a uniqueness that made it well acclaimed.

These references above point to the country of Cush—Meroitic Cush—and bring pictures to our imaginations. We see the Cushite sailors plying the Red Sea, the Mediterranean Sea, and the Indian Ocean in their ships made of bullrushes and loaded with exports of iron products, ebony, elephants, and jewelry; stopping at usual ports of call; unloading exports and reloading imports all along the way. The merchants and buyers and traders from various lands would be on hand to receive their shipments to be sold to customers. The people in all of the countries in the Old Testament world were familiar with these merchant seamen from the great African kingdom beyond Egypt. The merchants knew their products and the people knew their products; what they sold was in great demand, for their wares had a unique stamp: they were from Cush, and that insured the customer that his purchase was unique in its value. These sailors, no doubt, came ashore and mingled with the people. Many of them, it would seem, left the ships in order to remain, especially when beautiful maidens indicated a desire to be wed to them. They fellowshipped with the people, learned new languages and taught their own, and the children were thrilled and fascinated by these strange and wonderful men who could tell tall tales about the sea and about faraway places of the earth. The fact that the men were black was never an item of importance. They were ambassadors, messengers, seamen, bullrush-ship crewmen, bringers of iron, sellers of the famous topaz. All this, and only one man in the Old Testament indicates that they were black, and that indication comes in an analogy. If we need ask why there is no reaction to their color, we can answer our own question by remembering that a black man in Israel was a familiar sight. There were undoubtedly myriads of black Israelites, and there were black men marching in great armies, coming from various countries and empires, sailing ships, and traveling in chariots and on elephants. It seems possible to say that beyond the borders of the African continent, there has been no nation in the world history that was as familiar with the black presence as was ancient Israel.

We have seen the merchant seaman of Cush, but we must not lose sight of the overland caravans of traders who made the trek to and from the land of Cush, carrying with them various products representing many nations. Some of these caravans were Cushite caravans, but most of them would be men from other lands coming to exchange goods that were acquired in many countries along their route; these would leave Cush loaded with their exports to find markets all over the then-known world.

Alliances between nations are nearly as old as the nations themselves; it has been as if nationhood is too great a position for a nation to maintain by itself. The reasons that are given from time to time for forming these unions between nations range from mutual national security to a more profitable international trade. As we look back upon the cemeteries of dead nations, it is not clear whether alliances between nations have given life or have been one of the means of taking life away. George Washington, the first president of the United States, left a warning against becoming involved in European entanglements, but during the war he was ready to accept the service of the Hessians, Haitians and the French; so his warning did not specifically include having European nations involved in United States entanglements. The people of the Old Testament world set the pattern for those yet to come. They were great framers and makers of international alliances for the purpose of mutual defense and national expansion.

The nation of Israel did not bother to form alliances, military or otherwise, for a number of years after its beginning. Under the leadership of Moses, the nation had been organized and led all the way to the plains of Moab—actually to the banks of the Jordan River. Moses taught Israel to look to God who had a new name[1] but was the same God who had dwelt with Abraham, Isaac and Jacob; and the Israelites met with success in their mission under Moses. Joshua was also the kind of leader who taught his people to look to God and to themselves, and without assistance, he succeeded in conquering the land of Canaan. While it is true that Joshua was not able to subdue each and every Canaanite nation, he did take the mastery of overall Canaan and exhorted the tribal armies to clear out the pockets of resistance in their respective areas of assignment. When Joshua died, the Israelites had achieved nationhood because they now had a land of their own, one that they had taken from other people by right of the sword. Since that day, they have felt free to leave it or to be taken from it, later to return and take it again from whomever is in possession of it.

During the years of rule by the Judges, Israel kept itself free from all alliances. They were preoccupied with the task of national development and improving conditions of living for their families and their tribes. Ever so often during the period, some neighbor who was stronger would sweep in, take Israel's crops, put them to tribute and hold them under subjection; and in the process of time a "strongman" would emerge, and, depending upon God and his own people, would lead Israel through war to freedom. This sequence of subjugation and return to freedom occurred at least a half-dozen times during the years of the Judge's rule over Israel, and yet no one thought of or attempted to form any alliance with other nations. They remained a "go it alone" type of people.

The business of forming alliances did not begin immediately with the rise of the monarchy in Israel. King Saul was Israel's first sovereign, and his regime was devoted to the expansion of her borders. He was a man who has not been given full credit for his leadership. He was encumbered with the constant presence of the frustrated Samuel, who had been replaced as the leader and who dominated the king through religious intimidation. Just about everything that Saul did, Samuel said that God did not like; and, as might have been expected, King Saul almost lost his mind under the strain of so many national problems and the omnipresent Samuel the prophet. Saul is to be admired for having maintained a quiet, subservient, and respectful attitude towards Samuel at all times, because at times this must have been almost impossible. Imagine a situation such as is reported in the fifteenth chapter of the first Book of Samuel. There was Saul returning from a victory over his old enemy Amelek; the soldiers must have been rejoicing and the maidens might have met him with timbrels and dance, while the populace shouted their praise and admiration to the commander and his army. We see that Saul, when approached by a dour Samuel, said, "Blessed Be Thou of The Lord: I have performed the commandment of The Lord." Then with evident scorn Samuel said, "What meaneth then this bleating of the sheep in mine ears, and lowing of the oxen which I hear?" And for a moment we expect to hear Saul say, "What the Holy Ghost do you think it means?" but he does not say anything like that. He actually forgot for a moment that he was the king, and in an apologetic manner, he explains the people's actions to Samuel. King Saul tried to make his nation large and secure; he died in battle up on Mt. Gilboa.

Following the death of Saul, Israel did not concern itself with the making of alliances, because a seven-year civil war was required before the next king could be enthroned. The winner was David, of course, who had found political asylum with the Philistine king, but now set himself to the task of expanding Israel's borders and making those borders secure from invasion. The accomplishment of this mission made of David "a man of blood," but just before his death he turned over to his son Solomon a nation that was fully expanded, nationally secure, and free from interference from without. David's death brings to a close the long era in which Israel stood alone in the world, depending upon the one great ally—God!

The policy of forming alliances with other nations arose with the accession of King Solomon in Israel, and for him it became a major plank in his platform of foreign policy. Although Solomon always negotiated from a position of strength, he did not make it obvious in dealing with the neighboring kings. During his reign, Israel was geographically bigger than it had ever been or ever again would be. He commanded the biggest army in all Hebrew history and was also the builder of the first navy; but his foreign policy was based upon charm and diplomacy, and his alliances were cemented with sex appeal. He formed peaceful alliances with most of the kingdoms surrounding him in his day, and he sealed these relationships by marrying the daughters of the kings. He even married the daughter of the Egyptian pharaoh of his day, and her father conquered several Syrian cities and gave them to his daughter and son-in-law for wedding presents. From the time of Solomon, the Children of Israel were constantly forming alliances with other nations and other monarchs. This became one of the heavy burdens in the preaching of the prophets. Their voices in opposition to military alliances, once raised, were never hushed. They preached against these alliances saying that Israel had forsaken its dependence upon God and had begun to depend upon men whose arms and armies could not save the Israelites from destruction. In spite of the opposition of the prophets, Israel and later Judah still found it necessary to form mutual defense pacts with other nations, and destruction did come just as the prophets said it would; while above the noise and din of the aftermath to the Babylonian destruction of Jerusalem was heard the voice of Jeremiah telling what was left of Judah to make God the ally and not man. The Old Testament contains many incidents that reveal involvement of alliances between the Children of Israel and other nations, and among these allied nations is Cush, the African nation that was beyond the borders of Egypt and was given the name of Ethiopia by the Greeks who noted their "burnt faces."

In the days immediately prior to the destruction of the northern kingdom called Israel, there came an invasion led by King Shalmaneser of Assyria, who succeeded in overpowering his prey and putting them under tribute, the tax of the conquered. According to Shalmaneser's orders, Israel was obliged to pay sums of money to Assyria. In the language of the Old Testament, Hoshea became Shalmaneser's servant (2 Kings 17:3) and gave him presents, translated in the margin as "rendered tribute." Under such domination and in this subjugated condition, King Hoshea decided that he needed an ally to help him against the Assyrians, and he sent messages to King So, the Egyptian pharaoh. The Egyptian king must have in the past built up a reputation for responding to such appeals for help, because

King Hoshea of Israel was so certain that his appeal would bring help that he deliberately failed the Assyrian his yearly tribute. But alas, there was apparently no response to Hoshea from King So, so the King of Israel one day found himself bound in an Assyrian prison and his subjects transported into Assyria and other lands. This is known in Bible study as the depopulation of Samaria, and it signals the beginning of the Hebrew Diaspora. Shalmaneser took the entire Israelite population out of Samaria and scattered them around, and into that land he brought migrants from Babylon, Cuthah, Ava, Hamath and Sepharvaim. These new Palestinians were given one priest to teach Hebrew law and custom. They were, of course, never able to master Judaism in a manner that was satisfactory to Israelites; and because of this, there existed an estrangement between the Israelites and Samaritans forever. Also from this point onward, the northern kingdom of the Israelites ceased to exist, and Judah, made up of the tribes of Judah and Benjamin, became alone the state of Israel.

The King So of Egypt that is mentioned in the story is said to have been Shabako, whose dates are 712–700 B.C. He was the third monarch of the Twenty-fifty Dynasty of Egypt, which is the number of the Cushite dynasty. Some scholars claim to have found some Assyrian sources of information that would tend to make Shabako an Assyrian, but had this been true, then certainly Shalmaneser would have know it and Hoshea would have had better perception than to depend upon one Assyrian's coming against another. From the weight of the evidence, the great body of scholars have identified So as Shabako or (Shabataka) of the Cushite Dynasty, who was the uncle of the famous Taharka whose identity is not in doubt.

Unfortunately for Israel, Shabako or (So) must have had severe troubles of his own and could not come to their rescue. The mutual friendship must have been there, for it would not have been likely that Hoshea would depend so utterly upon an untried friend. He had to have had a somewhat feared reputation as a warrior, if for no other reason than that he was the brother of the famous Piankhy. It was Piankhy who had completed the conquest of Egypt, which conquest had been started by King Khasta. We must also admit the Hoshea of Israel might have thought that he was appealing to Piankhy himself, unaware that the throne had undergone a change of rulers.

There is possible reason to believe that some of the Israelites escaped before or during the destruction and depopulation of Samaria and that some of these escapees fled to Cush for sanctuary. This possibility is shown in some of the prophecy of Isaiah. Years before the Babylonian conquest of Judah, Isaiah was predicting that Assyria would invade both Egypt and Ethiopia (Kush or Cush) and that the conquest would be utter and the destruction would be severe. Isaiah talks about Israelite remnants that would someday return to Palestine the homeland, and among the returning remnants would be those who had been left in Cush.[2]

There was a black king of Egypt that became an ally to the King of Judah by coincidence, or even by accident. This refers to the famed Tikharka (Taharkah or Taharqa), whose efforts gave Judah a breathing spell at a very needy time indeed. In fact, it was he who saved the life of Judah for a little while, and one wonders what the final outcome would have been had Egypt and Judah been cemented into a mutual alliance. In this instance, the right man was on Egypt's throne, and more than likely he would have responded with an eager vigor that might have turned the tide.

Not many years after the northern kingdom, Israel, was destroyed, the same Assyrian monarch, King Shalmaneser, began to extend his power over Judah, which was ruled by King Hezekiah. Shalmaneser was able to attain domination over Judah, but King Hezekiah, was strong enough to rebel against him and to make the rebellion effective. So very confident was King Hezekiah, that he began to make some imperial moves of his own. He invaded parts of Philistia, perhaps with a determination to expand and strengthen his own nation and kingdom.

Eight years after the fall of the northern kingdom called Israel, Judah was threatened with invasion by one of the most noted warrior kings in Old Testament history. His name was Sennacharib (2 Kings 18:13), and he was King of Assyria. Hezekiah had submitted peacefully at first to Shalmaneser and had won the goodwill of his enemy with silver and gold. He used all the treasures in the king's house, and even gave away the gold from the decorations on the doors and that which overlaid the pillars. Hezekiah's submissive attitude is portrayed in a message sent to the Assyrian King: "I have offended; return from me. That which Thou puttest on me will I bear." He set about then to meet the demands of "the Assyrian wolf who came down in the night," which called for "three hundred talents of silver and thirty talents of gold."

After enduring the tyranny of Sennacharib for a while, Hezekiah apparently began to show signs of rebellion. We do not know what he did; but his actions were serious enough to stir the passions of the Assyrian king, for he sent a big army to Jerusalem. There were three big-name commanders with the Assyrian troops, but a Captain Rabshakeh seems to have done all of the talking. Hezekiah sent three emissaries to meet the Assyrian commanders who were stationed "by the conduit of the upper pool, which is in the highway of the Fuller's Field." The outspoken Captain Rabshakeh first sent his threat to sack Jerusalem to Hezekiah, but later he shouted out a similar threat in the "Jew's language." Rabshakeh had either a feeling or knowledge of the effect that Hezekiah's new-found nerve and courage might be based upon his confidence in an ally, and he felt that such an ally was the king of Egypt. He repeatedly told Hezekiah and the people that no God could save them from falling before his army, because in his belief, God had deserted when Hezekiah took down the high places and altars. In order to show the folly of trusting in Egypt, the captain devoted a part of his speech to the weakness of such an ally; he said: "Now on whom dost thou trust, that thou rebellest against me? Now, behold, thou trustest upon the staff of this bruised reed, even upon Egypt, on which if a man lean, it will go into his hand, and pierce it: so is pharaoh King of Egypt unto all that trust on him."[3]

The prophet Isaiah, by some manner, apparently knew something that Rabshakeh did not know. When Hezekiah sent counselors to ask his advice, Isaiah did not encourage surrender; he definitely encouraged defiance. His words were as follows: "Thus shall ye say to your master, thou saith the Lord, be not afraid of the words which thou hast heard, with which the servants of the King of Assyria have blasphemed me. Behold I will send a blast upon him, and he shall hear a rumor, and shall return to his own land; and I will cause him to fall by the sword in his land." Isaiah's prophecy came true. Rabshakeh heard a report that was more than a rumor—it was a fact; for before very long someone told the captain that the restless black warrior-king by the name of Tirhakah, King of Ethiopia (Cush) and Egypt had come to Assyria, looking for a fight.

His majesty, King Tirhakah (called Tirhakah in the Bible and Taharkah or Taharqa in historical sources), came to the Egyptian throne around 683 B.C. He must have been a busy expansionist, because the size of the kingdom seems to have broadened dramatically under his rulership. Historians have found that Tirhakah ruled almost a quarter of the African continent. His kingdom stretched from the shores of the Mediterranean to the borders of modern Ethiopia. His capital was the city of Tanis, which is located in the Delta region of Egypt, and it is said that he preferred this site for his capital so that he could keep a close watch on affairs in Asia Minor.[4]

Lerone Bennett, Jr., gives an appraisal of Tirhakah that should help us to understand just how highly regarded he is: "This resourceful leader left inscriptions which indicate that he conquered the Hittites and the Assyrians—claims which most Egyptologists discount.[5] His sway was so complete and his power was so absolute that he dubbed himself 'Emperor of the

world.'" Bennett cites another source considered to be "famous
Egyptologist," who called Tirhakah's reign "an astonishing epoch
of 'nigger' domination." A further quotation is taken from the
writings of a Dr. Randall-MacIver who says: "It seems amazing
that an African Negro should have been able with any sort of
justification to style himself Emperor of the world." It should be
stated that such a fact is amazing only in the Western world,
wherein black people have been cast mostly in the role of slaves
and wherein the myths that were used to condone the slave trade
and slavery always portrayed black people as lacking in civilization. But to the Old Testament and its world Tirhakah's claim
would not have been amazing nor would it have been received
with any doubt. The greatest powers that the Israelites of
Tirhakah's era ever saw were led by black warrior-kings who
were supported principally by black armies. Israel was accustomed to seeing black on top, so the Hebrew Bible does not even
bother to mention the color. It was the Greek biblical translators
who introduced the term describing color, and they were not
motivated by any tinge of bias. They used the term Ethiopian
merely because that is what they saw—black faces—faces whom
the Greek gods admired.

If either Tirhakah or Sennacharib ever defeated the other, it
was not recorded; however, we know that the Assyrian army and
Tirhakah's army began to clash in the Sinai desert area. Around
671 B.C. Egypt was attacked by Assyria, and Tirhakah was driven
back as far south as the City of Thebes. He was still strong
enough to mount a counterattack that drove the Assyrians
completely out of Egypt, but he could not keep them out. The
Egyptian army was encountering for the first time in world
history an enemy who used iron weapons, and the iron prevailed; the Egyptians under Tirhakah were permanently driven
back by the Assyrians under Esarhaddon. Tirhakah died in 663
B.C. and was succeeded by a nephew.

Tanwetamani (Tanutaman), successor of Tirhakah, immediately renewed the fight to recapture the City of Memphis, but upon

hearing of the approach of the iron-wielding Assyrians, he withdrew to Thebes. The Assyrians continued to press southward, and Tanwetamani permanently withdrew from Egypt and set up his capital in the Cushite city of Napata. The Assyrian army continued to press towards Thebes, and finally gave to Thebes a sacking that astounded the Old Testament world. The news reaches us through the prophet Nahum, as he thunders his prediction of Ninevah's destruction:

> Art thou better than populous No (Thebes), that was situated among the rivers, that had the waters round about it, whose rampart was the sea, and her wall was from the sea? Ethiopia and Egypt were her strength, and it was infinite; Put and Lubim were here helpers. Yet was she carried away. She went into captivity: her young children also were dashed in pieces at the top of all the streets: and they cast lots for her honorable men, and all her great men were bound in chains. (Nah. 3:7–10)

The Cushite monarchs retired from the throne of Egypt, but, as has been said, they went on to build the most glorious kingdom that inner-Africa ever produced. That their cooperation and exchanges with the Israelites persisted for many years is established in the New Testament Acts of the Apostles. Phillip the Apostle was by God sent southward over the desert road wending from Jerusalem to Gaza. Along the way he met what the Bible calls "a man of Ethiopia, an eunuch of great authority under Candace, Queen of the Ethiopians . . . ."

The use of the term "eunuch" is quite possibly misleading to the average Bible reader, who probably knows only one definition of the term, and that is a castrated male person. The term "eunuch" also means an officer of the court, or a chamberlain, which seems the better to describe a "man of great authority," who had come to Jerusalem to worship and was riding in a chariot. Also the term "Candace" is not a name, it is a title. The passage reads "under Candace Queen of the Ethiopians," but it really means "the Candace of the Cushites," for that was the title of the person whom Europe would call the Queen. So the story actually tells of a Chamberlain of the court of the Candace of Cush, who was sitting in his chariot reading from the prophecy of Isaiah. He was mystified and puzzled by the prophecy, and Phillip, always the evangelist, used this opportunity to preach Christ until the man was convinced and converted. Having come to Jerusalem to worship, the black Chamberlain must have been a Judaist in the first place. Either he was a convert to Judaism or he might have been a descendant of the Jewish remnant that fled from the destruction of Jerusalem by the Babylonians. In any case, the Cushite's presence in Jerusalem shows the continuing good will and exchanges between Israel and Cush.

It is to be said again and again that the Old Testament prophets seldom seem happy about Israel and her relationships with allies. They insist that international allies divert attention from the arm of God; that the military strength of these allies encourage the people actually to cease depending upon God of their Fathers. They preach that national security depends upon God alone working with the Children of Israel, because the greatest army in the world is but an arm of flesh that will be powerless when disaster strikes. The only instances in which the prophets speak favorably about anything pertaining to allies are those instances in which they are predicting the safe return of Jews who have sought refuge in allied lands. Zephaniah foretells the restoration of Jerusalem and the return of a remnant that will do no evil and speak no lies. They will have waited upon God, and Zephaniah hears God say (3:10), "From beyond the rivers of Ethiopia my suppliants, even the daughter of my dispersed, shall bring mine offerings." Isaiah 11:11–12 predicts that God will "assemble the outcasts of Israel, and gather together the dispersed of Judah from the four corners of the earth," and in the number he sees those coming from Cush.

When the prophets scold the Children of Israel about forming alliances, they include alliances with Cush as well as with Egypt. Isaiah 31:1 says, "Woe to them that go down to Egypt for help." On the other hand, when there is friendliness and cooperation between nations, the people of one can usually live in peace in the land of the other, and such instances are reflected in the Old and New Testaments concerning Israel and the Cushites. A Cushite was in David's army under Joab (2 Sam. 18:21). It was he who sped on foot to tell David that the rebellion had been quelled and that Absalom, the rebel son, was dead. There was a Cushite in Zedekiah's house (Jer. 38:7) who was so securely in the king's confidence as to be believed when he told the king that Jeremiah and his friends had done no wrong. Zedekiah believed Ebedmelech in spite of the fact that he had allowed the princes to cast the prophet into the dungeon mire. It was upon the advice of the king, made wise by his own testimony to him, that Ebedmelech took thirty men and lifted Jeremiah out of the dungeon and put him in the court prison instead.

Questions
1. When did Cushite rule end in Egypt?
2. How long did Meroitic Cush continue to exist?
3. Can you list some Cushite exports?
4. Of what materials were Cushite ships constructed?
5. What Cushite jewel is mentioned in the Book of Joab?
6. Under whose reign did Israel begin to form alliances?
7. Name the black warrior-king who became ally to Judah by coincidence.
8. Can you remember anything about King Tirhakah?
9. Do you know the meanings conveyed by the term "eunuch"?
10. Can you name the black man that rescued Jeremiah from the dungeon?

Notes
1. Exodus 6:2, "And God spake unto Moses, and said unto him, I am The Lord: And I appeared unto Abraham, unto Isaac, and unto

Jacob, by the name of God Almighty, but by my name Jehovah was I not known unto them.

2. Isaiah 11:11.

3. 2 Kings 18:21.

4. *Ibid.*

5. If Tirhakah left inscriptions that indicate his conquest of the Hittites and Assyrians, it seems that there could be no grounds for discounting his claim. The inscriptions were not private letters tucked away and hidden from his contemporaries. These were public inscriptions published before the very people that were involved in all his conquests; and if they did not dispute Tirhakah's claim, why should we discount it now?

10

PARTNERS UNDER DOOM

N HIS BOOK *The Territorial Imperative,* Robert Ardrey, the playwright turned anthropologist, teaches us that the territorial drive or instinct might possibly be mankind's oldest and most basic instinct and that it is handed down or up from his evolutionary past. This theory disagrees with the one held by a multitude of scholars for a long, long time; for it was once a settled question that the sex drive or instinct is the most basic drive in animal life. Mr. Ardrey gives the reason for the mistaken idea that has been held for so long by pointing out that those conclusions were based upon studies that were made by observing animals in captivity. Animals in captivity do not exhibit the territorial drive so very much, because the need for it is obliterated in their surroundings. Such animals have their territory to great extent; it is provided by the captors. Animals who spend their lives in their natural habitat, in the wilds and forests, must seek and win their territory and must be able to defend it for a lifetime.

The definition which is given for the term "territory" is "an area of space, whether earth or air, which an animal or group of animals defend as an exclusive preserve"; and it is said to take precedence over all other needs and desires. The author based his conclusions upon observing that animals in their natural habitat will not only fight and die defending their exclusive preserve, but he saw them faced with choices. For example, it was noted that an animal who finds himself facing the threat of losing either his mate or his territory will sacrifice the mate to save his preserve. Ardrey saw embattled animals make the choice, and he sees the same basic drive in human beings. We, too, show the territorial imperative in the same way and manner as do animals. It is mankind's first and basic instinct or drive to secure an defend his exclusive preserve. Mankind also wades into battle, hazards and loses life and limb in order to retain his territory, and when faced with a choice of losing it, will sacrifice everything else—sex, mate, friends, life. No other cause rallies armies and pulls human beings into battle like the territorial imperative. Among human beings the drive is called patriotism, national security, freedom, and independence; it might be called a group's right to life, liberty, and the pursuit of happiness. The defenders are universal heroes. Their acts and deeds fill a great portion of the pages of history, and a nation's songs, poetry, and prose tell endless stories of those who gave themselves and their all to defend the group's exclusive preserve. The Alamo and the Pass of Thermopylae appeal to the deepest instincts in human nature.

However, if the territorial imperative is mankind's oldest and most basic drive, then it is closely followed by the drive to intrude upon the territory of others—to conquer and to subject other people's exclusive preserve to the intruder's control. Just as soon as one man's exclusive preserve is somewhat secure, he begins to seek and find ways to gain ownership and control of his neighbor's preserve. The history of mankind is in large measure the accounts of groups of people seeking and achieving domination over other people and their lands. The drive to take ownership and control of other people's preserve is powered by many reasons or rationalisms. One group is able sometimes to teach its own members that their lives are unfulfilled merely because their neighbors are there. At other times, a group convinces itself that danger exists between themselves and others merely on the grounds that there *are* others. The long list of causes that have bred wars could be summed up by saying that as soon as one group achieves territory, they find reasons to need the territory of others. The reasons run the gamut of national security, political advantage, economic necessity, population pressures, and a host of others. It is to be noticed that in the world of 1974 A.D., Christianized, educated and supposedly dedicated men can convince themselves and their nation that a weak little peace-seeking group of people, ten thousand miles away, are a threat to national security; and the armies will march, the bombs will fall, and the navies will sail almost around the world. Here is living proof that the instinct to violate another's exclusive preserve is almost as prevalent and equally as strong in mankind as Ardrey's territorial imperative is in animals.

The anthropological evidence that points to mankind's earliest existence upon the earth does not picture them as members of ethnic, social, and political entities as large as nations or empires. On the contrary, the farther back we see, the smaller grouping of mankind seems to be. The indications of mankind's remotest past pictures them functioning in the family and the extended family groups: the same kind of groups that characterize the beginnings of the people called the Children of Israel. At a later stage, the groupings of mankind have grown larger through procreation and accretion—outside people have been taken in through intermarriage, capture, and some type of naturalization. As the telescope of anthropological research moves closer to the time of written history, the groups in which mankind lived are seen to become larger and larger, because it was during the early growth and organizing among human beings that wars began. Family groups began to conquer other family groups, villages began to conquer other villages, until there came into existence the political units that are called "states." With the rise of states, came the increase in the size of armies and the improvement in methods of warfare; and from this growth and development empires were born—one state was able to take control of the exclusive preserve of several other states. In many instances the conquered lost their language, their history, and their original identities. The empires themselves became great empires, lived and flourished until overcome by greater ones, or were smashed into pieces; and the pieces awaited another conqueror. The rise and growth of human groups from extended family size to empire proportions was accomplished by war. The political map of the world has always been modified by marching armies. The soldiers of the world have never ceased marching beyond the boundary limits of their own territory across the territory of their neighbors; and the enlargement of every boundary spelled the doom of a conquered nation. This has been a common fate, shared by all men on this earth. Virtually everybody's ancestors have been conquered by somebody else.

Preeminence among ethnic or national groups has been based upon the presence of different factors at different times. The unequal kindness of the elements of nature has played its part. At times the territory of one group has been blessed with land that was more fertile by the benevolence of nature, and because of such blessings the populations grew larger, wiser and stronger, while the death and disease rates were held somewhat in abeyance; therefore the stronger group has been able to overpower and to annex the territory of its weaker neighbors. At other times, such advantage as geographical location has been the factor upon which military superiority was based and built. Groups that have sat astride the natural trade routes have often been able to outgrow their neighbors through taxation, hijacking and plunder, and thereby have grown strong enough to march out and engulf the markets and resources of doomed trading partners and merge them into a much larger unit under their domination. In some instances, the hegemony of groups or nations was made possible by the discovery of metals and other treasures of the earth. Others have grown phenomenally strong because of the chance or labored invention of new and improved weapons. Had Assyria been obliged to use the conventional weapons of the day, Tirhakah might have reigned in Tanis until he was an old man and then might have turned the kingdom over to a son whose life span would equal his own. At other times, the presence of seas, oceans, rivers, and other waterways have been the greatest contributors to the hegemony of groups and have thereby been the cause of the rise and fall of many ethnic or national groups of mankind.

Judging from the history at hand, the rise and fall of nations and empires has been a vital and an inevitable part of the human story, and as far as human imagination can see ahead, this will continue to be true. The fall of nations and empires has been as certain as the rise of same. All the known territory upon the planet earth has been shifted from the control of some groups to the control of others. There is hardly a human being on this earth today who is part of the same nationally bounded group or empire that his ancestors belonged to two thousand years ago. For example, many Jews have returned to the land of Palestine and have built and established a free and independent country called Israel; but two thousand years ago, Judah, the predecessor of today's Israel, was an outlying possession of the Roman Empire. Two thousand years ago the nation of Cush was at its peak, sending merchant ships and ambassadors to the lively ports of the then-civilized world; but today that territory is a part of a nation called Sudan, and Islam, which was unborn when Tirhakah moved back to Napata, is the ruling religious and political force in the land. Less than two thousand years ago, the kingdom of Ghana was a large and flourishing empire; today that territory is called Mauritania, and it may be somewhat politically free and independent, but it is a part of the Muslim empire and a remnant of people, the Akan tribes, have placed the name Ghana maybe a thousand miles to the south to where the Fanti and Ashanti nations once lived in independent freedom. Mali is still Mali, but its empire is gone; European colonialism has come and gone, and Islam has made it a part of a new entity. The descendants of Assyrians, Babylonians, Persians, Greeks and Romans hardly know who they are, for the empires are gone, and in the shifting maze of rising and falling empires, the present day individual cannot say with certainty just who his ancestors were. The person today, living in the land that bears the name that it carried two thousand years ago cannot be at all sure just when his forebears went there or how. Some of the empires of history once seemed too formidable ever to fall, but they did. Some grew so large that the citizens thereof could truthfully boast that the sun never set on the empire, because the boundaries of their subjugated holdings followed the rotation of the earth from hemisphere to hemisphere; but such is not the case today or ever again will be for them. There have been those gargantuan-size nations and empires who freely used terms of endurance like "never" and "forever," but stronger groups arose without and within, and the power shifted. A Christian hymn composed by Bishop A. Cleveland Coxe asks the question, "O Where are Kings and Empires now, of old that went and Came?" The scholars of the world have filled many volumes digging out and setting forth facts to answer Bishop Coxe's question, but the most definitive answer is given in the nursery rhyme about the gingham dog and the calico cat that sat on the mantel. They too disappeared, and the same question was asked, Where did they go? The answer was, "They ate each other up."

The Old Testament is a veritable encyclopedia of the rise and fall of nations during the periods of history that are reflected in its pages, for the Old Testament world itself was the great arena in which a great deal of the cycle among nations and empires occurred. Everybody's armies won their share of victories, and many nations enjoyed their day of dominance. Conversely, everybody's armies met their share of defeats, and equally as many nations suffered their days of subjugation. Hegemony followed hegemony, and empires succeeded empires, rising and falling, rising and falling.

The prophets of the Old Testament were miracle men indeed. They did not have access to the kind of historical information that is available today. It was not there to be used. They had nothing to compare to the mass media of today in depth, breadth, or scope. There were no daily newspapers or newspapers of any kind setting forth the day-to-day actions and decisions of national leaders, both great and small. Nor did they have anything akin to radios and televisions to bring to the fore and to analyze national and international events as fast and as suddenly as they occurred. There were no literary men who specialized in making known and interpreting the design of some nations with respect to others. Their libraries were not filled with volumes by the thousands wherein people could find enough information with which to analyze everything about everybody; and upon the basis of such interpretations, predictions could never be made. Those Old Testament prophets knew a great deal, but they depended largely upon God for their deeper knowledge and revelations concerning their world. Yet with unerring accuracy, the prophets predicted the rise and fall of practically all the nations and empires in their turn throughout the history of the Old Testament times. They predicted the downfall of every great nation and empire whose name appears in the Old Testament except one—Rome; and St. John, the New Testament Seer of Patmas, followed the example of his Old Testament predecessors and, in coded messages, predicted the fall of Rome. Unto some nations the prophets said "Woe"; for others they said "It shall come to pass"; "The Lord will send"; or "I will punish saith the Lord."

The rise and fall of nations and empires went on before the prophets came on the scene, even before Israel was born; and they failed to predict the doom of these merely because they were not yet there. Had the prophets been there, they would have seen the southernmost of the Delta states, in the land which later became Egypt, spread its arms of dominance over the northernmost state and form the nation that became dynastic Egypt. They did, however, predict the fall of great Egypt, who was the mistress of the Old Testament world longer than the times of duration of all the other Old Testament empires added together. The prophets were not there when the great Hittite empire was spread over the areas of Mesopotamia, Syria and Canaan, but too many of the bits and pieces that were alive in their day, the prophets said "woe." The Old Testament prophets were not yet born when Egypt reached out her tentacles and drew Cush and Libya into her boundaries, but they had come to earth when both Libya and Cush reversed the order of conquest, and each of her turn took mastery over the mistress. The prophets missed the Hyksos oppression of Egypt and were not around when the Libyans drove them back into Asia, but they could have foreseen the events had they been on the scene. The Old Testament prophets had not been born when the Israelite juggernaut, under the leadership of Moses and Joshua, smashed its way into Canaan, displacing, killing, and oppressing the Canaanites in order to establish a home; but they had their say at a later date concerning later ventures by the descendants of these Israelites. The prophets predicted the fall of Israel, whose empire reached its peak during Solomon's reign, and, true to their prediction of doom, Israel's empire broke up into five distinct parts and pieces during the reign of Solomon's arrogant, dull-witted son, Rehoboam. In this disintegration, the ten tribes of the north became independent Israel; the southernmost two tribes became independent Judah; Moab, Edom, and Ammon regained their separate independence. The prophets foresaw the coming of the Assyrian host, who conquered everything between and including Israel and Theban-led Egypt. The prophets foretold, and one prophet went to jail for foretelling, that the Babylonian horde would smash and trample everything and everybody from Jerusalem to Thebes again. Also, the prophets of hope somehow knew, and let it be known, that Cyrus, "the Scourge of God," would lead the Medes and Persians in victories that would enslave the entire Middle Eastern world; yet he would grant semifreedom to Jerusalem, while pushing their way into the Egyptian Sudan to set their borders south of Napata. In a vision, the prophet Daniel (8:2–20) saw the rough goat with a great horn between his eyes, and to that extent he foresaw the day when the Greek king and commander, Alexander The Great, would gaze upon the dead body of Darius the Persian; would make the known world his conquered empire; and would weep because he could find no other worlds to conquer. Alexander would set himself up in oriental splendor and would later die the debaucher's death, leaving his once-great empire divided asunder by two of his closest associates. Historians can only wonder what the Old Testament prophets would have predicted had they lived long enough to see the furious rivalry between Rome and Carthage. They would have seen Hannibal, the black warrior, march in victory across Spain and lose somewhere around two-thirds of his troops, forcing men and elephants to cross the Alps so that he could claw down the gates of Rome. Twenty years passed, and the restless warrior could await advantage no longer; an ill-attempted attack upon the walled and impregnable city of Rome wrote "finis" to his career. The intertestamental prophets must have foreseen the coming of Rome, and perhaps knew that Rome would become master of the whole world as it was then known, spreading its armed Pax Romana over all Europe, Asia, and in the Sudan area that it called Nubia. The prophets would have been opposed the new religion called Christianity, a religion that would grow bigger than the empire and change the cross of Jesus from the symbol of suffering liberation into a symbol of conquest in Christ's name. The prophets might have welcomed the rising and flowing might of the barbarians who broke the Roman Empire into ruin, again allowing once-conquered nations to try to pull themselves together and live the lives of free nations. The prophets would have preached against the rise and lightening-like spread of the Arab-Muslim empire, which in less than a century-and-a-half had conquered half the world; who failed to conquer France after nineteen years of trying to do so; but who managed to put Spain and what became Portugal into the same empire that included the Philippines. The prophets may have foreseen that certain other nations would become world powers. They would actually find new land, greater in size than the land they already knew; they would spread all over the globe, conquering all of humanity, and they would send colonists into every nook and cranny of the earth. They would purchase and dehumanize some of the world's best-endowed people and sell them as slaves to lesser men, because they brought to the world a new criterion by which a man's worth and dignity would be measured—color! This new conqueror made skin color a new religion, as he became the "white man." He would place all other men in graded categories, putting black at the bottom of the scale and granting increasing human treatment as he dealt with groups who were lighter in skin color. Most of the "white man" colonies planted by yesterday's European powers have broken away from Europe's control. They now live in a world of tension because one fears the hegemony of the other. The Old Testament prophets are not around to tell us what will happen next, but all the prophets of today well know that the next step will take place, and all are pondering the question, what shall it be? What is next on the agenda of the "territorial impera- tive"—both phases of it?

The black powers of the world did not escape the wrath of the Old Testament prophets, for they were as active and as guilty of wrong as the others. They were flourishing in a day that was different from the modern era in that no combination of other powers submerged them from view because of color. The European was not on the scene, and so his peculiar talent for rapine had not castrated and dehumanized the blackman as he was to begin doing in approximately 2,250 years later. At least a half-dozen of the Old Testament prophets mad the black lands "partners under doom" with the other nations by their predictions; they predicted their fall also. They prophesied the doom of "Ethiopia beyond Egypt," and in some instances they actually named the enemy who would do the deed. In using the phrase "partners under doom," all of the nations and empires of the Old Testament world are involved.

Isaiah begins by predicting the downfall of Cush. He says (18:1): "Woe to the Land shadowing with wings, which is beyond the river of Ethiopia: that sendeth ambassadors by the sea, even in vessels of bullrushes upon the waters, saying Go ye Swift Messengers to a nation scattered and peeled." He here implies that these Cushites came while Judah was suffering from disaster, for he calls his own country "a nation meted out and trodden down." Isaiah could see also the end of Cush, for it was by means of personal experience that God taught him exactly what her end would be like. The Lord commanded Isaiah to walk naked and shoeless for three years until he was ready to understand. The Lord said: "Like as my servant Isaiah hath walked naked and barefoot three years for a sign and wonder upon Egypt and upon Ethiopia: so shall the King of Assyria lead away the Egyptians prisoners, and the Ethiopians captives, young and old, naked and barefoot, even with their buttocks uncovered, to the shame of Egypt. And they shall be afraid and ashamed of Ethiopia their expectation, and of Egypt their glory." (Isa. 20:3)

Such a scathing denunciation of Cushite-ruled Egypt by Isaiah the prophet is enough to make a student wonder just what Tirhakah had done to Judah. More wonder on this point is added when the student slowly reads the nineteenth chapter, the later part of which predicts that the tide will turn in favor of Judah. The Egypt that Isaiah talks about in this chapter was at that moment under the reign of the Twenty-fifth Dynasty, which is the Cushite dynasty, and Isaiah believed that the princes and the king's counselors were foolish and brutish; that perhaps they had advised that certain things be done for which Egypt must pay:

The burden of Egypt. Behold, the Lord rideth upon a swift cloud, and shall come into Egypt: and the idols of Egypt shall be moved at his presence, and the heart of Egypt shall melt in the midst of it. And I will set the Egyptians against the Egyptians: and they shall fight every one against his neighbor; city against city, and kingdom against kingdom. . . . And the Egyptians will I give over into the hand of cruel Lord; and a fierce king shall rule over them, saith the Lord of Hosts. (Isa. 19:11)

It has already been pointed out that Isaiah was right in his prediction, for a few years later Esarhaddon the Assyrian drove Tirhakah out of Egypt and devastated the capital, and the fierceness of the battle would have caused the taking of the many captives that the prophet foresaw.

In Isaiah's mind, the overthrow of Cushite-ruled Egypt was somehow ordained of God for the redemption of Judah, her partner under doom. The redemption or the redemptive process will bring about the exaltation of Judah. Isaiah 19:17 says: "And the land of Judah shall be a terror unto Egypt . . . In that day shall five cities in the land of Egypt speak the language of Canaan, and swear to the Lord of hosts: one shall be called the City of Destruction. In that day shall there be an altar to the Lord in the midst of the land of Egypt, and a pillar at the border thereof to the Lord." But Egypt shall also be healed, says Isaiah: "And the Lord shall smite Egypt: he shall smite and heal it:" For Cush there will be no escape from the king of Assyria (Isa. 20:6), but Israel, Egypt, and Assyria will co-exist peacefully (Isa. 19:24): "In that day shall Israel be the third with Egypt and with Assyria, ever a blessing in the midst of the land:"

Isaiah persisted in his belief that the overthrow of Cushite-ruled Egypt was a ransom for Judah's restoration. He again enunciates this belief in conjunction with one of the great texts of the Old Testament:

When thou passest through the waters, I will be with thee;
and through the rivers, they shall not overflow thee: when
thou walkedst through the fire, thou shalt not be burned;
neither shall the flame kindle upon thee. For I am the Lord
Thy God, the Holy One of Israel, Thy Savior: I gave Egypt
for thy ransom, Ethiopia and Seba for thee. (Isa. 43:2–3)

The prophet Jeremiah, writing approximately one hundred
seventy six years after Isaiah, foresaw Cyrus the Persian in the
same light. The first chapter of Ezra says that Cyrus fulfilled the
word of the Lord that came by the mouth of Jeremiah, and Isaiah
44:28 God, through Isaiah, said of Cyrus, "He is my Shepherd,
and shall perform all my pleasure: even saying to Jerusalem,
Thou shalt be built; and to the Temple, thy foundation shall be
laid." Cyrus is further called the Lord's anointed (Isa. 45:1). In
the Book of Ezra, King Cyrus confesses that "The Lord God of
Heaven hath given me all the kingdoms of the earth; and he hath
charged me to build him an house at Jerusalem, which is in
Judah." Isaiah, in foreseeing the day when Cyrus would rebuild
Jerusalem, predicts that Israelites in captivity and other captives
would return to Jerusalem to seek the Lord, and among these
captives are black ones. Thus saith the Lord (Isa. 45:14): "the
labor of Egypt, and merchandise of Ethiopia, men of stature shall
come over unto thee, in chains shall they come over, and they
shall fall down unto thee, they shall make supplication unto thee,
saying, surely God is in thee, and there is none else, there is no
God."

During practically the same span of years, both Jeremiah and
Ezekiel predicted the downfall of Egypt and the crushing defeat
of the Pharaoh. In a blaze of prophesy, Jeremiah identifies
Pharaoh-hophra (Jer. 44:30), who is said to have been Apries (or
Haaibra), the last pharaoh mentioned by name in the Holy Bible.
He is to be given "into the hand of his enemies, and into the
hand of them that seek his life." He will suffer the same fate of
Zedekiah of Judah. The prophecy is delivered against the reign

of Apries, but the total destruction of Egypt came during the reign of Pharaoh-Psamtik III (or Ank-ka-en-ra) by the armies of Persia; and when we hear of the Persians in Egypt, we remember that they pushed on to Napatan Cush.

About ten years following the capture of Jerusalem by the Babylonians, the prophet Ezekiel began to foretell the doom of Pharaoh, king of Egypt (29:2): "Son of man, set thy face against pharaoh king of Egypt, and prophesy against him, and against all Egypt." Nebuchadrezzar of Babylon, thought Ezekiel (29:19), would debase Egypt forever. Its people would be made captives, and later when allowed to return, they would be a base nation; and all of this will come upon the Egyptians because of their tendency to exalt the Nile, or perhaps worship the Nile. Ezekiel continues to see horror mount upon horror in the destruction of Egypt, and in spite of the fact that the Cushite kings have long been driven from the throne, leaving Egypt under the rule of the Saite kings, yet the people of Cush, says Ezekiel, will experience great suffering when Egypt's time comes to hand. Says Ezekiel (30:4): "And the sword shall come upon Egypt, and great pain (margin says fear) shall be in Ethiopia, when the slain shall fall in Egypt. . . ."

In that statement of prophecy, Ezekiel leads us to believe that many Cushites lived in Egypt and further strengthens belief that an alliance continues to exist between the two nations. Such an alliance is suggested in Verse 5 which says: "Ethiopia, and Libya (margin says Phut), and Lydia, and all the mingled people, and chub, and the men of the land that is in league, shall fall with them by the sword." The prophet had already defined the scope of Egypt's destruction (29:10) when he said, "Behold, therefore I am against thee, and against thy rivers, and I will make the land of Egypt utterly waste and desolation, from the Tower of Syene (margin 'or from Migdol to Syene') even unto the border of Ethiopia." The idea of the black alliance becomes a definite reality when the prophet at last speaks plainly about it:

Thus saith the Lord: they also that uphold Egypt shall fall; and the pride of her power shall come down: from the tower of Syene shall they fall in it by the sword, saith the Lord God. And they shall be desolate in the midst of the countries that are desolate, and her cities shall be in the midst of the cities that are wasted. And they shall know that I am the Lord, when I have set a fire in Egypt, and when all her helpers shall be destroyed (margin says "broken"). In that day shall messengers go forth from me in ships to make the careless Ethiopians afraid, and great pain shall come upon them, as in the day of Egypt: for, lo, it cometh. (Ezek. 30:6–9)

The prophet Zephaniah closes his vision of the Israelites' tomorrows with a beautiful picture of a restored remnant:

The remnant of Israel shall do no inquity, nor speak lies; neither shall a deceitful tongue be found in their mouth: for they shall feed and lie down, and none shall make them afraid. Sing, O daughter of Zion; shout, O Israel; be glad and rejoice with all thy heart, O daughter of Jerusalem. The Lord hath taken away thy judgements, he hath cast out thine enemy: The King of Israel, even the Lord, is in the midst of thee; thou shall not see evil anymore. (Zeph. 3:13)

Before this blessed condition can come to pass, according to Zephaniah, God will bring destruction upon many lands and places. Wickedness will be the cause of God's destruction, and it is to visit Jerusalem, Maktesh, Gaza, Ashkelon, Ekron, the Cherethite Nation, Canaan, the Phillistine nations, Moab, Ammon, Assyria, Nineva, and the Isles of the heathen. And, as is expected, he does not leave out Cush (Zeph. 2:15): "Ye Ethiopians also, Ye shall be slain by my sword." Of course, we must restate the fact that Zephaniah saw Cush as having been a land of refuge for some of the Israelites of the Diaspora, for they too would come back home again to worship (Zeph. 3:10): "From beyond the rivers of Ethiopia my suppliants, even the daughter of my dispersed, shall bring mine offering."

Finally, Daniel was the man who could foresee the coming of the Greeks under Alexander the Great, and his vision foresaw the man's conquest of the Persian Empire and of the world. The prophet appears to have known beforehand that following his death, Alexander's kingdom would be rent into sections (Dan. 11:3): "And a mighty king shall stand up, that shall rule with great dominion, and do according to his will. And when he shall stand up, his kingdom shall be broken, and shall be divided towards the four winds of heaven; and not to his posterity." Daniel also describes great battles and destructions by and between "the King of the North" and "the King of the South," and he appears to know that in the years of battle between the descendants of Seleucus I and those of Ptolemy Soter, a descendant of Seleucus, Antiochus Ephiphanes,[1] would rule the Cushites along with the Jews. The prophecy says: "He shall stretch forth his hand also upon the countries and the land of Egypt shall not escape. But he shall have power over the treasures of gold and of silver, and over all the precious things of Egypt: and the Libyans and the Ethiopians shall be at his steps."

As the Old Testament closes, we see the partners under doom in the world of its day, including Judah and Cush, marching together, unwillingly, towards the valley of the shadows. The New Testament shows that they survived and found new heights of glory and freedom—more so with Cush than with Judah—and the valley of darkened shadows returned. Today there is a renewed Israel, struggling determinedly to find a secure place among the nations of the world, and the Cush of yesterday is now a part of the Republic of Sudan, with a newly found independence and freedom. Will the territorial imperative keep them alive, or will mankind's desire to violate another's territory again send them to doom?

Questions

1. What is the "territorial imperative" as explained by Robert Ardrey?
2. Why did Ardrey call the territorial imperative mankind's oldest drive?
3. What other drive is said to follow closely the territorial imperative?
4. Are there any people on earth whose ancestors have never been conquered?
5. A part of what empire was Judah at the birth of Christ?
6. In whose empire was Cush at the time of Christ?
7. Upon whom did the Old Testament prophets depend for wisdom?
8. Isaiah believed that the overthrow of Cushite-ruled Egypt was a ransom for whom?
9. What prophet foresaw Hebrew supplicants returning from beyond the borders of Cush?
10. Did Daniel foresee the downfall of a black nation?
11. In what modern country is the ancient land of Cush now located?

Notes

1. Frederick C. Eiselen, Edwin Lewis and David G. Downey, Eds., *The Abingdon Commentary* (Nashville: Abingdon Press, 1929).

BIBLIOGRAPHY

Aptheker, Herbert. *Afro-American History: The Modern Era.* New York: The Citadel Press, 1971.

Ardrey, Robert. *African Genesis.* New York: Dell Publishing Co., 1961.

Ardrey, Robert. *The Territorial Imperative.* New York: Dell Publishing Co., 1966.

Bennett, Lerone, Jr. *Before the Mayflower.* Baltimore: Penguin Books, 1962.

The Holy Bible. Authorized (King James) Version.

Bohannon, Paul. *Africa and Africans.* New York: The Natural History Press, 1964.

Brawley, Benjamin. *A Social History of the American Negro.* London: Collier-Macmillan Ltd., 1921.

Breasted, James Henry, and James Harvey Robinson. *History of Europe Ancient and Medieval.* New York—London: Gin and Co., Ltd., 1929.

Chamberlin, Roy B. and Herman Feldman. *The Dartmouth Bible,* Boston: Houghton Mifflin Co., 1950.

Coughlan, Robert, and the Editors of *Life, Tropical Africa.* New York: Time Inc., 1962.

Davidson, Basil. *Africa Genius.* Boston-Toronto: Little, Brown and Co., Atlantic Monthly Press, 1969.

Davidson, Basil. *Africa: History of a Continent.* New York: The Macmillan Co., 1966.

Davidson, Basil. *Africa in History.* New York: The Macmillan Co., 1968.

Davidson, Basil. *African Kingdoms.* New York: Time Inc., 1966.

Davidson, Basil. *The Black Mother.* Boston-Toronto: Little, Brown and Co., 1961.

Eiselen, Frederick C., Edwin Lewis, and David G. Downey, ed. *The Abingdon Commentary.* Nashville: Abingdon Press, 1929.

The Encyclopedia Americana. New York: American Corporation, 1953.

Franklin, John H. *From Slavery to Freedom.* New York: Alfred A. Knopf, 1947.

Gadd, K.M. *From Ur to Rome.* London: Ginn and Co., Ltd., 1936.

Gunther, John. *Inside South America.* New York-London: Harper & Row, 1966.

Harman, Carter, and the Editors of *Life. The West Indies.* New York: Time Inc., 1963.

Hastings, James. *Dictionary of the Bible.* New York: Charles Scribner's Sons, 1907.

Herodotus. *History.* Trans. George Rowlinson. Great Books of the Western World. Chicago: Encyclopedia Britannica, Inc., 1952.

The Horizon History of Africa. Ed. Alvin Josephy, Jr., *et al.* New York: American Heritage Publishing Co., Inc., 1971.

Howe, R.W. *Black Africa.* London: New African Library, 1966.

Jordan, Winthrop D. *White Over Black.* Williamsburg: The University of North Carolina Press, The Institute of Early American History and Culture at Williamsburg, VA, 1968.

Josephus, Flavius. *The Antiquities of the Jews.* Trans. William Whiston. Grand Rapids: Kregel Publications, 1960.

Kraeling, Emil G. *Historical Atlas of the Holy Land.* New York: Rand McNally Co., 1959.

Lands and Peoples. New York-Toronto: The Grolier Society, 1929.

Lincoln, C. Eric. *The Negro Pilgrimage in America.* New York: Bantam Books (updated and expanded edition), 1969.

MacGregor, Geddes. *The Bible in the Making.* Philadelphia: J.B. Lippincott Co., 1959.

Murphy, E. Jefferson. *History of African Civilization.* New York: Thomas Y. Cromwell Company, 1972.

Parrinder, Geoffrey. *Religion in Africa.* Baltimore: Penguin Books, 1969.

Pope-Hennessy, James. *Sins of the Fathers.* New York: Alfred A. Knopf, 1967.

Purchas, Rev. Samuel. *Hakluytus Posthumus or Purchas His Pilgrimes,* Vol. I. Philadelphia: Rare Books Department, Free Library of Philadelphia.

Quarles, Benjamin. *The Negro in the Making of America.* London: Collier-Macmillan Ltd., 1964.

Redding, Saunders. *They Came in Chains.* Philadelphia: J.B. Lippincott Co., 1950.

Sandburg, Carl. *Abraham Lincoln.* Especially Vol. I, *The Prairie Years.* New York: Charles Scribner's Sons, 1926.

Seligman, C.G. *The Races of Africa.* London: Oxford University Press, 1966.

Shinnie, Margaret. *Ancient African Kingdoms.* London: Edward Arnold Publishers, Ltd., 1965.

Smith, George A. *The Book of Twelve Prophets.* London: Hodder and Stoughton, 1902.

Smith, William. *Dictionary of the Bible.* Teacher's Edition. Philadelphia: The John Winston Co., 1884. Revised and edited by Rev. F.N. Peloubet and M.A. Peloubet.

Tacitus, P. Cornelius. *The Annals* and *The Histories.* Trans. Alfred John Curch and William J. Brodribb. Great Books of the Western World. Chicago: Encyclopedia Britannica, Inc. 1952.

Tenney, Merrill C., *et al,* editors. *The Zondervan Pictorial Bible Dictionary.* Zondervan Publishing House, 1963.

Terrien, Samuel. *The Golden Bible Atlas.* New York: Golden Press, 1957.

Werblowsky, R.J. Zwi, and Geoffrey Wigoder. *The Encyclopedia of the Jewish Religion.* New York: Holt, Rhinehart and Winston, 1966.

Wiedner, Donald L. *A History of Africa South of the Sahara.* New York: Random House, Vintage Books, 1962.

INDEX